THE CRIN

Crime and Society
Soc 3910 - Handbook

Colin Francome

MIDDLESEX UNIVERSITY
COURSE READERS

First published in 1997 by Middlesex University Press

Middlesex University Press is an imprint of Middlesex University
Services Limited,
Bounds Green Road, London N11 2NQ

A CIP catalogue record for this book is available from
The British Library

ISBN 1 898253 13 7

Manufacture coordinated in UK by Middlesex University

The Crime Solution

TABLES

BIBLIOGRAPHY

The Crime solution

Introduction

When the Conservative Government took office in 1979 it was as the party of 'law and order'. In this respect it is instructive to recall some of Lady Thatcher's comments at the time. She said that under Labour *'there would be no new attempts tackle crime'* (Wightman 1979c p36). This she contrasted to the efforts which the Conservatives would make. To a Scottish audience she said:

I know how acutely worried you are about the crime wave and thuggery. I give you this assurance: under a Conservative Government there will be no neutrality in the war against crime. The challenge that the vandal and the hooligan pose to the well being of each one of us, old and young and the civilised standards on which all depends will be met and repulsed with the utmost determination (Wightman 1979a p36).

Her method of combating crime is outlined in a 1979 newspaper report in the Daily Telegraph. It said that Mrs Thatcher stated as follows: *'There must be a great stress on the need to uphold law and order in society,'* The report continued:

'She went on to say that this could be done by having enough police, by ensuring the Government's backing of the police and the Government's recognition of judges being wholly impartial in the way they carry out the law' (Wightman 1979b p36).

In the next two chapters we will be examining the evidence in some detail to see how successful was the 'war against crime'.

The rise in crime 1979 to 1992

In fact despite the rhetoric crime was a major growth industry. This is true whatever measure is taken and in the next chapter several alternatives are considered. However, the result cannot be denied that the government in power since 1979 has been unsuccessful in combating crime. It is true that not all crimes have risen every year and that in some years there have been reductions in some offenses. However, the overall position has considerably worsened. The total number of crimes recorded by the police rose from 2.5 million in 1979 to 5.6 million in 1992 (Table 2.2).

One possible explanation for the increase was the rise in inequality. We know that during the 1980s and early 1990s the government followed very right wing policies. It reduced income going to the poorest sections of the community, reduced the real value of child benefit and privatised companies. This allowed the new owners to give themselves large salary increases while in some cases reducing the money going to their workforce. So one possible explanation of the increase in crime may be seen as a result of a set of policies designed to move the country to the right.

A second possible explanation-the one favoured by some right wing thinkers- is that the decline in stability of the family is the cause. These explanations will be considered in more detail together with other possibilities.

The mixed statistics 1993-5

The politicians statements may have indicated a great reduction in crime during this period. The Prime Minister John Major claimed in the House of Commons in January 1996 that his policies had resulted in *'the biggest fall in crime for more than 40 years'*. Similarly his Home Secretary Michael Howard has continually stated that there has been a down turn in crime and that this is due to the fact that his tough stance on sentencing, prisons and police powers is working (Rose 1996 p1). These comments are based on the overall number of offenses recorded by the police which fell from 5.6 million in 1992 to 5.5 million in 1993, 5.3 million in 1994 and 5.1 million in 1995. So at one level there has been a welcome fall. However, there are a number of words of caution that should be heeded. The first point is that at these levels the rates of crime are still more than twice as high as when the administration came into office in 1979. However, the main reason that these statements were unduly optimistic was that they ignore the fact that more serious crime had continued to increase. Mr Major's comment, for example, came just two months after figures for 1994 were published showing that Britain had the highest number of 'Crimes initially recorded as homicide' since the late 1850s, the highest rate of recorded rapes and an increase in the in the number of crimes of violence.

Furthermore, although the figures for 1995 which were published in March 1996 did show an overall fall, again we must treat the change with caution and a number of points should be considered.

a) Although they showed an overall 2.4 per cent fall-the third year running they had fallen. There were, however, reports that the number had bottomed out in the latter part of the year and might now begin to rise once again. Home Secretary Mr Howard was asked whether he felt this to be true. He commented:

'I am not here to predict, I am here to report. I cannot guarantee that every set of figures I produce will follow the downward trend we have established. It is very encouraging that the figures reveal the third annual fall for only the third time this century. The other occasions were 1913 and 1952-4' (Travis 1996).

We can agree with the Home Secretary's implication that there are problems with taking year on year figures as being as a result of policy changes. However there are other issues.

b) One is that even excluding the possibility that the fall was all in the first part of the year, the comment of Mr Howard was unduly optimistic. It was the lesser crimes that had fallen. The data also showed a 14 per cent increase in street robbery, a two per cent increase in violent crime and that for the second year in a row the number of homicides rose to an all-time peak this century. The rapes of rape at 9.9 per 100,000 in 1995 are threatening to rise over 10 per 100,000 for the first time ever.

<u>Reasons for the levelling off in some crimes</u> We saw above that one suggestion for the recent fall in the crime rates is due to the increase in prison population. This was criticised by Paul Cavadino who suggested that in the last six months of 1995 both the prison population and crime rate rose together. There is also the problem that prison may deter the less serious offenders but act as a 'crime academy' for more serious offenders (Travis 1996). If this were true, and it is far from proven, then it could help explain the continuing increase in the more serious crimes.

A second explanation for the fall in crime could be the reduction in the unemployment rate. The relationship between poverty, unemployment and crime will be discussed in chapter nine. A third explanation, suggested to me by a well known popular journalist is that people have stopped reporting crime to such a degree because they know that in many cases it will cause themselves trouble but not lead to arrests. This again is speculation but some of the problems with analysing trends in crime are discussed more fully in chapter two.

A fourth possible explanation is that the crime prevention measures are having an increasing effect. The installation of closed circuit television on the London Underground reduced muggings and theft (Shepherd and Farrington 1995 p272). Banks, supermarkets and shopping markets have all introduced similar measures and the identification on video of the murderers of young James Bulger gave great publicity to the effectiveness of these measures. It would be surprising if potential wrongdoers did not take such factors into account. Some observers call this the 'situational prevention of crime' and they point out that in some circumstances there can be displacement of crime. For example, when there was a campaign against street crime in one area of New York City, there was an increase in the surrounding districts:

'Similarly, a fall in thefts of newer vehicles fitted with steering locks was accompanied by a rise in thefts of older vehicles not fitted with such locks (Shepherd and Farrington 1995 p272).

In Britain the displacement of crime from the more visible places may have diverted it to streets where surveillance is less likely and also the offenses are less likely to be reported.

So there are a number of competing explanations which may have had some effect.

Structure of the text

This book aims to examine the facts surrounding the change in crime levels, to introduce students to some of the main ways of thinking of criminologists, activists and politicians; to examine the reasons for the changes in levels of crime and to make proposals which will help to reduce the rates. It is therefore in four parts. The first section considers the changes in crime and makes some comparisons. The second part examines different perspectives on the changes in level and the third section makes a more detailed analysis of certain selected topics. Finally some proposals to reduce crime are put forward.

In addition to giving students an introduction to criminology this book also aims to move away from the traditional criminological text books in the following ways:

A) Understanding all perspectives Young and Lea noted that there were two opposing views of crime. The right wing who saw 'that the war against crime is of central concern' and the left who sought to minimise the problem of working class crime (Lea and Young 1993 p11). Their book was an attack on the latter position and in general the debate amongst criminologists during the 1980s and early 1990s was often between the left and the extreme left. However, the political realities were of a debate between the right and the extreme right. It is in the hope that criminology can be made even more politically relevant that this book considers both the views of the far left and the far right in some detail.

So it considers the attitudes towards crime from various differing perspectives. In order to bring out the variations clearly I have identified six focal points which will serve the basis of comparison. These are as follows:

A) Attitude to major social institutions.

B) Attitude to the family.

C) Attitude to the role of the police.

D) The role of punishment.

E) Attitudes to crimes without victims

F) What is the solution to crime?

The differences between the groups on these issues are quite marked.

B Variations in crime levels Any theories of crime need to be able to explain the wide differences in reported crime rates between societies, regions, ethnic groups and the sexes. The epidemiological factors rapidly render visible the weaknesses of simplistic theories of crime. For example anyone who puts the case that murder is simply due to the wickedness of the individual would have to explain why people in the USA commit at least eight times as many murders per head of population as those in Britain.

6

<u>C Terrorist, guerilla or freedom fighter?</u> An important area of crime normally ignored by criminologists is that of 'terrorism'. However, it affects all our lives on a regular basis with the times taken to check in at airports being much longer these days and news programmes being regularly filled with the actions of deviant groups. Deviancy theory has much to offer as a method of explanation of these groups and so criminologists have potentially a great contribution to make.

The world is still a very violent place with great numbers of people being in situations of conflict. There are also many people who are concerned about the possibility that atomic and nuclear weapons will eventually fall into the hands of guerrilla groups who are opposed to dominant societies. These people who are often willing to be martyrs for their cause may well have far less restraint than exercised so far by the major governments. The British Medical Journal reprinted an important editorial from the <u>Economist</u>:

'Did you stop worrying about nuclear obliteration when the cold war ended? Start again. To make an atom bomb a terrorist or a would be proliferator would need to get hold of only 5 Kg of weapon-grade plutonium or 15 Kg of weapon grade uranium, less than you would need to fill a fruit bowl. At present the world probably contains about 250 tonnes of this sort of plutonium and 1500 tonnes of the uranium. To lose one bomb's worth from this stock is the equivalent of losing a single word from three copies of the <u>Economist</u>.... and more than half the world's stock of nuclear explosive material is inside the chaotic relic of the former Soviet Union' (Smith and Leaning 1993).

So there is an urgent and strong need for the world to move as far away as possible from international or even civil confrontations. I will be raising the issue of terrorism and make some beginnings towards an explanation.

Crime as normal

Many people take the view that crime is an evil, its elimination should be of primary concern and that this can be achieved by catching and punishing wrong doers. However, there have been at least two groups of commentators who have seen crime as being 'normal' behaviour.

a) Functionalists Durkheim argued that every single society has always had crime and because of this it is useless to talk of crime as an evil-*'this is the preacher's language not the scholars' (1915 p362)*. But Durkheim did not only argue that crime was bound to occur, rather he argued that because it always occurred that it must be in some way necessary for society to function:

No people exists whose morality is not daily infringed upon. We must therefore call crime necessary and declare that it cannot be non existent, that the fundamental conditions of social organisation, as they are understood, imply it. Consequently it is normal (p362)

He continued to argue that crime is useful but that it is only of value when it is reproved and repressed. It is normal that crime should occur and also normal that such crime is punished. So Durkheim's functionalist perspective led him to see some positive aspects of crime in terms of the functioning of society.

b) The Marxists Those in this tradition may also argue that crime is a normal adaption to capitalism because these societies are fundamentally unequal. However, in contrast to Durkheim they look to a future society where property crime at least would disappear. For example Jock Young argued:

Property crime is better understood as normal and conscious attempt to amass property than it is understood, for example as the product of faulty socialisation (1975 p34).

He continued to argue that society stressed self aggrandisement through the accumulation of property and that some did this by legal means and others by illegal means. So Young saw crime as a fundamental feature of all capitalist societies and, as there are currently no really Marxist societies, then crime must be normal everywhere.

The United States theorist Richard Quinney takes a similar position and put the position clearly:

'Only with the collapse of capitalist society and the creation of a new society, based on socialist principles, will there be a solution to the crime problem (1975 p199)'.

Developing an approach to Crime

We can agree with commentators that crime will not be eliminated in an industrial society but it is likely that we can reduce its incidence. The wide differences in rates between societies indicates that this is possible. So we must consider the social context of crime.

One matter of concern is that with the rising rate of crime the increase in preventative measures can lead to 'blaming the victim'. Those who do not always lock their car or who walk out late at night should be criticised for their actions. There is always a balance to be drawn, however, I take It is not an unreasonable expectation that people should be able to walk out late at night without fear of attack. As people cannot always currently do this there is a strong case for saying we should be considering where our socialisation is going so badly wrong that people have to take so many precautions.

The same really applies to property. There are societies where people do not have to spend a great amount of their time locking and unlocking doors and setting and releasing burglar alarms.

Indeed there are areas of Britain where this is still possible. However, at the moment they are few and far between as we shall see from regional burglary rates. So this course will in part be calling for a revaluation of values.

Chapter 2

Changing rates of Crime

There is only one measure of crime that comprehensively deals with the term of office of the administration in power since 1979 and this is the number of notifiable offenses known to the police. It may not be the best measure and there are problems of under reporting, however, the figures are striking. In 1994 there were 5.3 million offenses recorded. This is a rise of 2.8 million over the figure of 2.5 million in 1979 and so crime more than doubled over the period even allowing for a small population increase.

In 1983 the Home Office made a projection of ten years ahead, that is for the crime rate in 1993. It estimated that there would be 4.15 crimes known to the police in that year. This figure was passed in 1990 three years ahead of schedule. In the book <u>Law and order five years on</u> published in 1986 Lea, Matthews and Young predicted that the 1993 figures would be in the region of six million. In 1991, when there was an annual increase of 8.9%, it looked as if they might well be right. Indeed if that trend had continued the number of offenses would have been 5.8 million in 1992 and 6.3 million in 1993. In the event, however, this high rate of increase was not sustained and the number of crimes rose only to 5.5 million.

However, one point they make is that since 1979 there has been a vast increase in expenditure on law and order. In real terms it rose from £3.2 billion in 1979-80, to £12.9 billion in 1979-80. So it has quadrupled over the period. As part of this expenditure the number of police officers increased by 15% (1977-78 to 1989-90) and considerable prison building has taken place. In the private sector alone at least £1 billion was spent on security equipment, and as much again by local authorities. The expenditure by the private sector on security has increased. Other developments such as neighbourhood watch have stressed security and by 1993 had encompassed 3.5 million households. So the rise in crime must be seen in the context of the extraordinary measures taken to combat it.

<u>Caution about crime statistics</u>

Below we provide further figures for the latest numbers of notifiable offenses known to the police. Of course this will be an underestimate of the full picture. There is a complicated relationship between true and recorded crime. For a crime to be recorded it needs first to be recognised as such, secondly someone needs to think it sufficiently worthwhile to report it to the police and then the police must believe it is sufficiently important to record. Chris Lewis suggests that in the period up to 1992 there were improvements in the reporting and recording of crime (1992 p17). One factor leading to more crime being reported in urban areas is that the police are usually more easily contactable. Furthermore the improvement in communication with an increased number of telephones has meant that it is easier to contact the police in recent years.

So there are problems in knowing both how many crimes have been committed and also in changes over time. Lewis commented:

'Most criminal incidents are not clear cut events. A group of three men with knives might attack another group of five men at a bus stop, injuring two of them, robbing all of them of ready cash and stealing all their credit cards which are passed on and used to buy goods. There is room for discussion as to how many offenses have been committed. To cover such complexities and ensure consistency the Home Office issues Counting Rules to define how many crimes arising from such incidents are to be recorded (1992 p17).

There is also evidence that different offenses are reported to a variable degree and that over a period of time the reportage rate of some crimes may increase. For example, if the proportion of the population carrying insurance for house contents increased then it could lead to burglary being more often reported to satisfy the claims department of the insurance company. In fact the percentage of burglaries reported to the police appears to have risen from 75% in 1979 to 87% in 1985 but since then has remained constant or possibly slightly fallen (Foster et al 1995 p44). The message to the media from the police of improved treatment of rape victims and the increased willingness of the force to take the problem seriously is undoubtedly one fact leading to more women being willing to come forward and report the crime.

One of the problems in comparing crime trends over long periods is that changes in society make new goods available. A major source of crime now is theft of or from motor vehicles. These would not have occurred in the last century. Similarly thefts of televisions could not occur in the 1930s, thefts of videos would not have been possible in the 1960s and computer crime rare until recent years. So economic development brings the possibility of new crimes. There is also the added economic problem of inflation. There has been a cut off point in the criminal statistics of £20 for theft and criminal damage. As the vast majority of all offenses are property crimes and some of the items are very cheap, there is a danger of increasing crime as inflation increases the number of goods worth twenty pounds.

Improved medical care could also be a factor in the extent of homicide. Although we have seen that in 1995 there were the highest number of crimes recorded as homicide this century, the rates were much higher in the middle of the nineteenth century. They reached a peak in the late 1860s when they were around 18 per million population. They then steadily fell to seven per million at the end of the first world war-well below half the rate of fifty years earlier. In large part this improvement would have been due to better social conditions but another factor was undoubtedly improved medical care. The introduction of anaesthetics and knowledge of the need for cleanliness in treatment meant that many knowledge of the need for cleanliness in treatment meant that many people who were injured would have their lives saved. It was not until the 1880s that doctors began to wash their hands before operating for example (Francome et al 1993 p31).

There may also be changes in the law or in the application of the law. This applies in particular to the whole area of crimes without victims. Attempted suicide, homosexuality and abortion have all been legalised-at least within certain conditions. So there will be a reduction in crime in these areas. There are also many crimes to which the police turn a 'blind eye' in modern society but to which they might have taken a different view in the past. As late as the nineteen fifties the birth of a baby outside marriage was regarded by the vast majority of the population as an unfortunate occurrence. However, the improved levels of contraception and availability of abortion have meant that a young pregnant teenager now has a choice whether or not to continue the pregnancy. This change has probably been a factor in increasing the possibility that the police will take a lenient view to under age sex even if the man is over the age of twenty one. The available figures suggest that this has occurred.

Refer Table 2.1

The table shows that the conception rate amongst teenagers under the age of sixteen rose from 8.6 per thousand to 10.1 per thousand between 1985 and 1990. This suggests that under age sex was increasing or at least was more visible in the sense that the number of maternities increased by 32 per cent. However, the number of offenses of under age sex recorded by the police actually fell by 20% over this period. Over the period 1985-1993 the conception rate for under sixteens has remained relatively constant with an overall fall of only six per cent. This suggests that under age sex has not declined taking into account the increased efforts of birth control agencies like the Brook Advisory Centres. However, over this period the number of offenses of under age sex recorded by the police has declined by almost a half (46%).

Another victimless crime to receive more lenient treatment is the possession of cannabis which the police have increasingly been ignoring if the amounts are small enough to be for the persons's own use.

Road traffic offenses are another area where it is difficult to measure infringements in large parts of the law over time. The question of speeding in cars is another area where the police could take a much stricter line. Although the speed limit is 70 mph on motorways, the police practice is normally not to prosecute unless the person has exceeded 85 mph (Personal communication). Consequently it is 'normal' for motorists to exceed the speed limits in many parts of the country. Furthermore the police have come to expect that people will exceed the 30 mile an hour speed limit in some urban areas and have been known to stop people keeping to the limit and ask them why they are travelling so slow. One large change since the 1960s is in the police attitudes to bicycles. At one time they were very critical of people riding on pavements. As far as the young are concerned nowadays they take the view that the increased danger on the roads means that it is probably safer if this occurs sometimes.

The other side of this coin is that society might well take a more serious view of an action in recent years. At one time rape within marriage was not a crime but in recent years the law has been changed and other forms of domestic violence are also less acceptable these days.

Population structure is another factor. As males aged from thirteen to twenty three are more likely to commit crimes, an increase in the size of this age group is likely to raise the crime rate. In fact during the late 1990s this group will fall in size and so if other things remain equal the crime rate will fall.

Official Crime statistics have consistently shown that the working class and certain ethnic groups are recorded as carrying out more crimes than the national average. Jock Young in an article 'working class criminology' made a number of points. First, crime amongst all groups is overwhelmingly property crime. With more than seven out of eight crimes in the USA and more than nineteen out of twenty in Britain being of this nature:

'It is clear, in fact, that the vast bulk of offenses for which working class people are imprisoned or punished in Western societies have to do with the fact that, by virtue of being working class or black, they are without property' (1975 p35).

A second point is that those in charge of the society are likely to ignore the 'white collar' crimes. He drew attention to comments from a former Attorney General of the USA that illicit gains from such crimes far exceeded profits from other crimes combined. That just one price fixing agreement gained more illicit cash than all the burglaries, and thefts in the whole nation while it continued. Furthermore, bank embezzlements cost ten times more than bank robberies each year (1975 p35).

He suggested two values of the statistics. First they measure the extent that different groups are committed to the social order and secondly they can be used as evidence of the degree that the upper classes are pursuing different groups in the society.

Evidence from victim surveys

Instead of simply recording the number of crimes we can estimate the number by asking people about their experience in 'victim studies'. Since 1972 the General Household Survey has included a question on burglary with loss. Until 1979 the percentage of households that had been burgled in the last twelve months had remained more or less constant at 2.4%. It then began to rise to 2.6% in 1985/6, 3.5% in 1991 and 4.6% in 1993 which is the latest information (Foster et al 1995 p44). The General Household Survey showed some variations in the likelihood of being burgled. The age of the head of the household is important. In 1994 where the head was aged 16-29 the rate was 91 whereas where the head was over the age of 65 it was only 35. White people were less likely to burgled than members of ethnic minorities. They had a rate of 50 per 1000 households compared to 119.

The General Household Survey found a contribution in that those who were more likely to be burgled were the less likely to report it. Only 79% of offenses where the head of the household was aged under 30 reported the offence compared to 88% of those aged 65 or over. Similarly, although ethnic groups were more than twice as likely to be burgled, only 80% reported the crime compared to 88% of white people (Foster et al 1995 p46). It is possible to make a few comparisons based on data provided:

* Households in metropolitan areas were 43% more likely to be burgled than those in other areas.

* Compared to the heads of household being aged 16-29 those aged 30-64 had only 68% of the risk and those aged 65 and over had 41% of the risk.

* Homes in other parts of Britain had much greater risks of burglary compared to Wales. Those in Scotland had 1.9 times the risk, those in the Midlands and East Anglia 2.9 times the risk, those in the South 3.4 times the risk and those in the North 4.7 times the risk.

* Compared to single adult households those in two adult households had 73% of the risk and those of three adult households had 67% of the risk.

The BCS first reviewed crime in 1981 and therefore came too late as a measure of crime under the administration which has been in power since 1979. There were other surveys in 1983 and 1987 and the last one published referred to 1991. Like the others it was based on a representative sample of 10,000 people aged sixteen and over. The strength of such surveys is that they pick up crimes which people for a variety of reasons have not reported to the police. Such crime surveys do, however, have a number of drawbacks.

1 Many crimes such as commercial burglary, white collar crimes such as fraud and other crimes such as shoplifting cannot be adequately covered. This may have been particularly important in recent years as companies have become increasing privatised. Those involved in crime often use the argument that it is not so damaging to steal from wealthy companies as they make enormous profits so can afford it. Indeed some maintain that firms allow in their profit margins for a certain amount of theft. This situation has changed for many areas of the economy that were in state ownership. In the past people may have been constrained from defrauding the telephone companies on the grounds that they would be stealing from everyone and it would results in higher call charges. Now it might seem that they were simply stealing from a few rich people who had made enormous profits from the purchase of shares at well below market prices.

2 People will be reluctant to report certain categories of crime. The whole area of 'crimes without victims' will be very much under reported as there is no complainant. People will be reluctant to tell researchers that they visited prostitutes, supplied heroin or engaged in sex with a minor. So this whole area of offenses is likely to be very much under reported.

3 Homicide clearly cannot be included in a victim study. However, the British Crime Survey also took the view that sexual offenses

were likely to be inaccurately reported. So for this reason and to help improve the response rate sexual offenses were not included (Home Office 1995 p5).

4 The sample may not be representative. Young people who commit and suffer a disproportionate about of crime are usually under- represented in sample surveys. This is because they are more likely to be transient and so less contactable. In addition to these structural factors certain Government changes may well have compounded the situation. The impact of the poll tax was very important in making young people reluctant to talk to government agencies and the data from the 1991 census was known to be inaccurate. Furthermore the policies of excluding the young from certain benefits is also likely to have alienated many who would therefore be less likely to respond than hitherto. Consequently, those interviewed may well be increasingly the more 'respectable' people who would be better protected against crime. So again the Crime Survey may well underestimate the increase in crime.

5 In 1991 a different method of sampling was used. The Post Code Address File was used instead of the Electoral Register. This may make long term comparisons difficult, although the authors claim that no correction was needed because of this change (Home Office 1995 p7).

6 There may be differential counting between social groups. The 1994 British Crime Survey commented, for example that better educated respondents are more likely to report certain kinds of assault. They may be more likely to regard a crime as being within the definitions of the survey.

7 The British Crime Survey stated that in times of rising crime the increase may be underestimated:

It may be that frequent victims will be more likely to forget trivial incidents, leading to a relatively greater under count of crime.

(Analysis) suggests that an affect of this kind may have occurred (Home Office 1993 p6).

8 Sample surveys are sometimes inaccurate as can be seen by the mistakes sometimes made in predicting election results.

However, even with these reservations it may be that for a range of crimes against individuals and their property the British Crime Survey produces the clearest results. Young and Lea report that the results from the United States where victimisation surveys began to be used earlier have shown a close correlation between the increase in crime as measured by data from victim surveys and from crimes recorded by the police (1993 pix). So, although the statistics presented below need to be treated with some caution, there is no doubt that the levels of crime have risen substantially since 1979.

Refer Table 2.2

The results show that the number of crimes more than doubled between 1979 and 1994. Crimes of violence have increased from 119 thousand to 312 thousand. This is a 262 per cent rise. In 1994 crimes of violence reached a new peak with a rise of 6 per cent over 1993. The number of robberies has increased nearly five times during the Conservative's years of office. They rose from 12.5 thousand in 1979 to 60.0 thousand in 1994. The absolute figures indicate the amount of police work needed, but they do not take account of population changes and so it is a better indicator to take the rate of crime per 100,000 population as in the following table:

Refer Table 2.3

The results show that overall during the period of the administration since 1979 there has been a doubling of the crime rate per head of population. In 1993 and 1994 the overall figure shows there has been a slight reduction, however, the fall has been in the less serious crimes. The number of offenses of violence against the person rose to an all time high at 427 per 100,000 population which was a rise of 7% on 1993 and contrasts with a figure of only 193 in 1979. The number of sexual offenses rose to new heights but the increases were not as marked as with violence against the person (Home Office 1995 p44). The Home Office carried out an analysis for the years 1984-94 and during this period the more serious offenses increased at a substantially faster rate (11 per cent per year) than the less serious ones (6.5 per cent per year) (1995 p32).

The results show that the 205,000 recorded cases of violence against the person were 4% of all recorded notifiable offenses in 1993. The Home Office, however, commented:

Figures from the 1994 British Crime Survey indicate that violent crime increased at a faster rate than recorded crime. The survey showed that violent crime rose by 14% between 1991 and 1993 compared to a rise of 12 per cent in offenses recorded by the police. Since 1981 violent Crime as measured by the BCS has increased by 39 per cent whereas police figures show a rise of 115 per cent (Home Office 1994 p31).

There is another possible source of measure of violent crime. This is the number of victims of violence attending accident and emergency units. The number of victims attending one trebled during the period 1974-91 (Shepherd and Farrington 1995 p271).

As well as an increase in violent crime there has also been a remarkable increase in robberies in recent years. In 1991 they rose by 25 per cent, in 1992 by 17 per cent, in 1993 by 9 per cent and 1994 by seven per cent. Although robberies only account for one per cent of all notifiable offenses they showed a 77% increase over the five years 1989-94.

Over the ten years up to 1993 domestic burglaries rose by and average of five per cent a year. However, evidence from the British Crime Survey shows a smaller rise which suggests that part of the increase might well be due to an increased tendency to report the crime (Home Office 1994 p33). One good point about the statistics for 1993 was that there was a fall of one per cent in domestic burglaries, although burglaries of commercial premises rose leading to an increase in burglary by one per cent overall. The fall in domestic burglaries in 1993 was the first annual fall in five years and there was a greater than ten per cent fall in the City of London and Gwent. The reduction of crime in the city may have been because of the great increase in security linked to the IRA. One quarter of burglaries resulted in no goods being stolen, either because the attempt was not successful or because theft was not the reason for the break in. There was also a welcome fall of eight per cent in domestic burglaries in 1994 (Home Office 1995 p44).

Almost half of all notifiable offenses are 'theft and handling stolen goods'. These rose for the five years up to 1992 but then fell by 3% between 1992 and 1993 and by a further 7 per cent in 1994. More than half the thefts are of or from a vehicle. In 1993 the thefts from vehicles fell by 4 per cent, although the actual theft of vehicles rose by 1 per cent.

<u>Local differences in crime</u>

There are forty three regions in England and Wales but the figures for the City or London are included with the overall figures for the Metropolitan Police Area to give and overall total supplying data as forty two. Four of these areas are in Wales. The figures should be treated with caution and we shall see that the figures for Nottinghamshire are generally high, although victim surveys do not show such a high level as compared to other areas. It might well be due to the assiduous recording of the local police (Lewis 1992 p17).

The police force areas with the highest rate of notifiable offenses recorded by the police in 1994 was Humberside with 15,357 per 100,000 population, Nottinghamshire 14,837 and Cleveland 14,609. Some people think London has a high crime rate but the Metropolitan Police including the City of London had a rate of 11,633 which is only 14% above the average for England and Wales. The lowest rate was in the Welsh area of Dyfed-Powys with a rate of 4583 which is only a third of that of Nottinghamshire. Other low rates were Hertfordshire 6465 and Wiltshire 6543.

There were regional differences in violence against the person. Nottinghamshire recorded the highest rate of 750 per 100,000 population and the Metropolitan Police (including the City of London) was second at 632 in 1994. The lowest rates were in Lancashire at 227 per 100,000 population, Hertfordshire 235 and Sussex 238. Nottinghamshire also had the highest rate of sexual offenses with 111 per 100,000 population followed by the Metropolitan Police at 94 and Gloucestershire 86. The Nottinghamshire figure is over three times that of Hertfordshire and North Yorkshire with 36 (Home Office 1995 p43). These figures indicate that those areas with high rates of violence in general have high rates of sexual offenses and vice versa.

The Met had the highest rate of robbery in the country with 347 per 100,000 population which is three times the average of 117 in England and Wales and thirty eight times the rate of the lowest police district. Second highest was the West Midlands with 267 and third Greater Manchester with 208. The lowest robbery rate by far was Dyfed-Powys with a rate of 9 per 100,000, followed by North Wales and Cumbria 15, and Gwent and Suffolk on 18. The overall robbery rate for Wales was only 22 which is less than a fifth of the rate for England (122) (Home Office 1995 p43). The Welsh rate for sexual offenses was also lower than England, however, rates of violence against the person were slightly above the average.

The places with high rates of violence are not necessarily those with high rates of other offenses. Let us take burglary for example. In 1994 the Metropolitan area had a rate of 2227 per 100,000 which is below that rate of 2452 for England and Wales. The highest rate of burglary was Humberside with 4971 per 100,000 which is more than twice the national average. The second highest was West Yorkshire 4158 followed by Northumbria 3959 per 100,000 population. Like robbery the lowest rate of burglary was Dyfed Powys with 741 per 100,000 population. So residents of this area have only one seventh the burglary rate as those in Humberside.

The average rate of 'theft and handling stolen goods' for England and Wales was 4978 in 1994. The highest rate was in Cleveland 7673, Humberside 7072 and Nottinghamshire 6998. The lowest rate was Dyfed-Powys 2051, Suffolk 3037 and Hertfordshire 3391.

The General Household Survey published in 1995 contains regional information on burglaries. Yorkshire and Humberside had the highest rates with 87 per 1000 households. East Anglia had the lowest rate for England with 18 per 1000. The overall rate for England was 58 per 1000 which compared to 26 in Scotland and only 11 in Wales. So the average for Wales was only one fifth of the average figure for England (Foster et al 1995 p45).

Refer Table 2.4

The results show that in 1979 the clear up rate for crime was 41%. Crimes for which people are prosecuted but found innocent are still regarded as 'cleared up'. It fell to an all time low in 1993 and then rose slightly in 1994 when it was 26%. This was on slightly fewer overall crimes and in absolute terms the number of 'clear ups' was slightly lower in 1994 than in 1993. In 1979 the total number of notifiable offenses cleared up by the police in England and Wales was just under a million. They rose to a peak of 1.48 million in 1991 but have fallen in each successive year to 1.33 million.

In 1994 the lowest clear rate was the 17 per cent for criminal damage followed by burglary which was 21 per cent. The highest clear rate was for 'other notifiable offenses'. The second highest clear up rate was for violence against the person at 77 per cent followed by sexual offenses where the figure was 76 per cent. The clear up rate for theft in 1993 was 24% but varied according to kind. Less than one in ten (9 per cent) of thefts from the person were cleared up contrasted with four out of five (78 per cent) of the thefts from shops. Although the latter figure is clearly high because shops will usually not bother to report to the police unless the person is apprehended.

Within the national rate there was variation between areas and in fact three of the four Welsh forces recorded clear up rates in excess of 50 per cent in 1994 (Home Office 1995 p32).

Evidence from the British Crime Survey

We have outline some of the advantages and disadvantages of the British Crime Survey (BCS) including the fact that they do not stretch across the whole of the time period for the Conservative administration. However, Home Office estimates from the British Crime survey suggest that only about half of all offenses are reported to the police and only about a third or a quarter are recorded by them (Home Office 1995 p27). For some offenses the BCS recorded rises less than the increase indicated by Crimes recorded by the police. This was the case for violence against the person. However, for other offenses the opposite is the case. For example between 1983 and 1991 the BCS found that the number of domestic burglaries had risen by 134 per cent compared to a rise of only 108 per cent recorded by the police (1995 p33).

If we take the British Crime survey as accurate for a point of comparison it is possible to calculate a clear up figure:

Refer Table 2.5

This experimental table suggests that the high clear up rate for violence against the person is only so high because many are not reported.

Homicide since 1979

This includes the offenses of murder, manslaughter and infanticide. Murder and Manslaughter are common law offenses which have never been defined by statute. Manslaughter is the killing of another without any malice either expressed or implied. The Infanticide Act (1922) created the offence of infanticide *'in the case of a woman who caused the death of her child under twelve months while the balance of her mind was disturbed by reason of her not having fully recovered from the effects of giving birth to the child or by reason of the effect of lactation consequent upon the birth of the child.'*(Home Office 1994 p223)

The offence of causing death by dangerous driving is not usually covered under homicide, although the Dutch take a different general line on this issue. In 1993 there were 292 offenses of causing death by dangerous or careless driving and a further 17 offenses of causing death by aggravated vehicle taking.

When measuring homicide the offence is recorded as the year in which the offence was initially recorded by the police, which is not necessarily the year in which the incident took place which could have been some time earlier, nor the time of the court decision which was likely to be later.

Refer Table 2.6

In 1987 there were 72 homicides due to shooting which was 12 per cent of the total. The number then fell until in 1993 it rose again and there were 78 homicides which represented 13% of all homicides in that year (Home Office 1994 p72).

The results show that the number of homicides originally reported have remained relatively constant over the period 1979 -1993. The lowest post war figures were those of 261 in 1958, 265 in 1961 and 266 in 1959. The last time the number was below three hundred was 1965 and the last year the figure was below 400 was 1970 when it was 396. The highest number ever was in 1995 followed by 1994 and 1991 (Home Office 1994 p 76, Travis 1996a p4).

Method of killing

Refer Table 2.7

Table 2.7 shows that overall the most common method of killing was by use of a sharp instrument, followed by 'hitting and kicking' with strangulation being third. There were differences between the sexes. The most common method amongst females was strangulation (28%) and this accounted for slightly more than use of a sharp instrument (26%). The most common method of homicide for men was the use of a sharp instrument and this was the method in two in five (41%) of cases. Second most common method was 'hitting kicking etc', and third highest was shooting. Only eight per cent of the male homicides were by strangulation.

Comparison of 1994 with 1993 shows there were falls in the percentage killed by a blunt instrument, hitting and kicking and shooting. In 1995 there was a moral panic over the use of knives after a head teacher was stabbed outside his school just before Christmas. He was subsequently voted BBC's **Today** programme's 'man of the year'. The figures do seem to indicate that the concern was in part justified. The number of people killed by a sharp instrument was only 89 in 1969. It rose to 191 in 1979 and was still only 183 in 1993 (Home Office 1980 p192). However, it jumped to 236 in 1994 which was the highest ever figure and a 29% increase on the previous year. (Home Office 1995 p79) This

27

figure suggests that there may have been an change in the availability of knives and the willingness to use them. The rise particularly affected men and the increase was from 97 in 1985 to 154 in 1987 and then fluctuated until in 1994 it rose to 165 (Home Office 1995 p79).

Refer Table 2.8

The results show that 54% of male victims were acquainted with the suspect contrasted to 81% of the women. This is in large part due to the difference in likelihood of being murdered by a 'spouse, cohabitant or former spouse or cohabitant'. Over a third (34%) of women were murdered by a current or ex spouse compared to only four per cent of the men. In 1993 15 women compared to 78 men murdered their spouse. In addition a number of people were killed by their lover or former lover. If we add the two categories together then we see that 40 per cent of women and six per cent of men were killed by a current or former lover.

The likelihood of being murdered varies according to age. In 1994 the highest rate per million people is for those under one year old. This group had a homicide rate 42 and 1994 was the first year since 1982 that more baby girls had been killed than baby boys. The second highest age group was for those aged 16-29. In this age group the death rate for men was twenty three and for women it was eighteen. The lowest rate was for the age group 5-16 years when it was only four per million. In the age group 30-49 men were more than twice as likely to be murdered as women with the overall rate for the group being sixteen deaths per million population.

The reasons for homicide are not always possible to determine especially where the suspect has not been found. However the data over the past five years shows that as far as the murder of an acquaintance is concerned in just over three cases out of five it was due to 'quarrel, revenge or loss of temper'. This was also the reason for a quarter of the homicides by strangers (Home Office 1995 p83).

Homicide in the USA

The number of murders increased from 19,300 in 1983 to 24,500 in 1993 at which rate it was 9.5 per 100,000 population. In 1992 the murder rate for white males was 9.1 and for white females it was 2.8. So white women had only a third the chance of being murdered compared to white males. The murder rate for black men was 67.5 and so was seven times the rate of white men. Black females had a rate of 13.1 per 100, 000 population. The persons arrested for murder and non negligent homicide also showed an ethnic bias with 58 per cent being black and forty one per cent white.

It seems in the USA that murder has become increasingly a delinquent problem. During the period 1981-90 the number of juveniles (under 18) arrested for murder and manslaughter increased by 60 per cent compared to a 5 per cent rise in those over this age (Shepherd and Farrington 1995 p371). The proportion of all murders by the under 18s during this period increased from 9.4% to 13.6% (Shepherd and Farrington 1995 p317).

In the USA in 1993 seventy per cent of the murders were by shooting, thirteen per cent by cutting or stabbing, five per cent were by hands, feet etc and two per cent by strangulation.

Homicide in South Africa This has been called by the newspapers the 'murder capital' of the world. The murder rate reported at 61 per 100,000 population is well above that of second highest figure of 22 per 100,000 at the Caribbean Island of St Lucia. A report in July 1995 announced seven hundred arrests in what was described as a crack down on crime. The high crime levels are seen as a bar to economic growth and social stability (Beresford 1995).

<u>Homicide by a lone person</u> Some multiple murderers such as Nielsen and West commit their crimes over a period. Others, however, commit their crimes during a single day or incident and it is these which we are going to consider. In April 1996 a lone gunman killed thirty six people in Tasmania which was believed to be the worst ever massacre by a lone killer at one time. This led to the London <u>Evening Standard</u> (29 April 1996 p7) listing previous examples and I have placed the most recent first:

* Dunblane, Scotland February 1996: Thomas Hamilton killed 16 children and their teacher before committing suicide.

* British Columbia 1996: Man shot dead 9 members of a wedding party.

* Toulon, France 1995; A sixteen year old killed some relatives and shot 8 more.

* Gujarat State, India: 1994 A man doused wedding guests with petrol killing sixteen.

* San Francisco 1993: A man walked into a law firm and shot dead 9 people before killing himself.

* Kileen, Texas 1991: A man drove his truck into a restaurant before opening fire on customers and killing 22 people. He then shot himself.

* Aramoana, New Zealand 1990: A 'gun mad' loner killed 11 people before being killed by police.

* University of Montreal, Canada 1989; A 25 year old war movie fan shot dead 14 young women then killed himself.

* Luxiol, France 1989: A farmer shot dead 14 people. He was captured.

* Melbourne, Australia 1987: A man killed eight people before plunging to his death.

* Russelville, Arkansas 1987: A former US air force sergeant killed 14 relatives on Christmas Day.

* Melbourne, Australia 1987: A failed army cadet killed seven people after a barmaid rebuffed his advances.

* Falun, Sweden 1987: An army instructor shot at a group of young women killing 7 people including five women.

* Palm Bay, Florida 1987: A retired man killed six people including two policemen because 'a boy had walked on his lawn'.

* Bogota, Columbia: 1986 A Vietnam war veteran killed 30 people in six hours before being shot by police.

* Edmond, Oklahoma: 1986 A postal worker killed 14 people before killing himself.

* San Diego, California: Teenage girl shot dead 11 people saying she did not like Mondays.

* University of Texas: 1966. Student shot and killed 14 people after murdering his wife and mother. He was shot dead.

These eighteen cases of murder show clearly the importance of guns. The only real exception was the arson murder in India.

Prevalence of rape Scully suggests that between 25 per cent to 50 per cent of rapes are unreported. In one study of 246 victims of rape in Seatle who contacted a rape crisis centre 100 had not reported their rapes to the police. She also suggests that women are more likely to report the rape if it is of the classic kind where a total stranger invades a woman's home or attacks her in a public place (Scully 1991 p6). She therefore comments:

Rapists in prison, then, are more likely to have raped strangers, used weapons, physically injured their victims, and committed other crimes in addition to the rape(Scully 1990 p7).

This figure by Scully is likely to be conservative. In 'Sane New World' I commented:

One point to bear in mind is that the official figures are a gross underestimate of the number of rapes. Researchers estimate that only about one in five are reported and I would be inclined to put the figure lower than this. I have known six women who were raped and one of these was working in a drugs project in Brooklyn and was raped twice in a short period of time. The second occasion happened in broad daylight and she did not tell anyone- not even the man she married- for over five years. I would suggest a reportage rate of about one in eight in Britain and a lower figure in the United States, maybe one in twelve (Francome 1990 p100).

There are two reasons for expecting a lower reportage rate in the US. First many of the rapes occur amongst women in minority groups who are alienated from the police. Secondly the clear up rate for rape in the US is only just over half compared to four out of five in Britain. Going to court is a very harrowing experience for the rape victim and very often the evidence is not believed (Francome 1990 p100). A British doctor gained wide publicity in November 1988 when he claimed that one in three allegations of rape is false. Dr Gillian Mezey of the Maudsley hospital commented that the remark had undermined the attempts of psychiatrists and volunteers working with women to convince them that it was worthwhile reporting attacks and that their claims would be believed. She drew attention to a New York study which found the rate of false allegations to be only two per cent which is comparable to unfounded complaints in other criminal offenses (Francome 1990 p101).

There is no doubt that rape and other violent attacks against women are a great problem. A study in the Islington area of London by Jayne Mooney published in 1987 found that in terms of non sexual assault, women were 40% more likely to report attacks compared to men and that one woman in five knew of a female who had been attacked in the previous twelve months. This was despite the fact that women took many more precautions than men. They were, for example, five times more likely to never go out after dark, three times as likely to avoid certain people or streets and six times more likely to always go out accompanied rather than alone (Francome 1990 p101).

In Britain young white females are twenty-nine times more likely to be assaulted than those over the age of 45 and 30 times as likely to be sexually attacked.

In the United States the national data show that two in five women do not feel it is safe to go walking most places at night. Johnson calculated the lifetime risk of rape to women aged 12 and over. He conservatively estimated that 20 to 30 per cent of young girls aged twelve years will suffer a violent sexual attack during the remainder of their lives. He said that such a common occurrence cannot be based on the behaviour of small minority and commented:

'Instead the numbers reiterate a reality that American women have lived with for years: sexual violence against women is part of the everyday fabric of American life (Johnson 1980 p146).'

The data for 1986 showed that in the USA women aged 16-19 were more than thirty times as likely to be raped as those over the age of 35 and that black women were twice as likely to be raped as white women. In part this latter figure may be the results of poverty as women with incomes under $7000 are fifteen times as likely to be raped as those with incomes over $50,000 a year (Francome 1990 p102).

The USA data also show wide variations in rates of rape over the country. In 1993 the highest rate was in the State of Alaska with 84 per 100,000 population, followed by Delaware (77) Michigan (71), Washington (64) and Nevada (61). The lowest rate was in West Virginia (20) followed by North Dakota, Connecticut and Iowa all with a rate of 24 per 100,000. So statistically a woman in Alaska has four times the possibility of being raped as one in West Virginia (**US in Figures** 1995 table 310).

Official statistics on rape

Refer Table 2.9

The results show the large increase in the number of rapes recorded in Britain. During the period 1973 to 1981 the rates were relatively stable only increasing from 2.0 to 2.2 per 100,000. Since that time, however, the recorded rates have more than quadrupled. So much so that in Britain during the period 1977-87 rape was the fastest growing crime in Britain.

The rates of rape as measured by Crimes known to the police rose by four times in the United States between 1960 and 1986. However the increase in rape in the USA has not been as great in percentage terms as that in Britain. In 1979 the rates of rape in the USA was fourteen times the British rate but in the most recent year (1993) for which comparable figures are available it was only four times as high per 100,000 population.

Refer Table 2.10

In 1995 there were 5,069 cases of rape reported (Travis 1996 p4). The increase has continued which led the Home Office to comment:

The number of rape rose by 10 per cent or 450 offenses in 1994, although in percentage terms this is less than the previous ten years. Much of the increase over this period is however, thought to be attributable to both an increase in reporting by the public and change in police practice resulting in an increasing proportion of the cases reported being recorded as offenses (1995 p32).

Some countries have much lower rates of rape. The Japanese, for example, record only a third as many rapes per head as the British (Francome 1990 p100).

The growth in use of weapons

The number of offenses in which firearms were used was only 685 in 1969 and 715 in 1970. They rose to 2466 in 1973 when only 32 were used in homicide (Home Office 1979 p 65 and 1993 p52). Table 2.12 shows the situation since 1979.

Refer Table 2.11

The results show that the number of offenses in which firearms were used doubled between 1979 and 1993 and then fell by 7 per cent in 1994.

Three quarters of the weapons used in 1969 were airguns. However, increasingly not only were more weapons used but also they were more often of the more dangerous kind. This was so much the case that by the time of the peak in 1993 less than half (45%) were airguns. In 1994 there was a welcome change in that there was not only a reduction in the number of offenses in which firearms were used but the percentage of more serious weapons also declined as air weapons become became more likely to be used and accounted for 55% of all offenses. There was a 29 per cent reduction in the use of pistols and a 26 per cent reduction in the use of shot guns in offenses. Offenses of robbery in which firearms were reported to have been used were down by nearly a third from 5900 in 1993 to 4100 in 1994.

Crimes without victims

The changes in the law during the Labour Government 1964-70 might have been expected to reduce the level of measured crime. The legalisation of homosexual activity for consenting males over the age of twenty one decriminalised a great amount of behaviour as did the further reduction of the age of consent for men to eighteen years. In addition the Abortion Act 1967 which came into operation on 27 April 1968 meant that the numbers of illegal abortions fell (Francome 1984). The more liberal attitude towards the possession of marijuana is also likely to have reduced the percentage of cases prosecuted.

European comparisons

Although virtually all countries collect crime statistics absolute comparisons are difficult to make and will be affected by very many factors. There are for example, different legal and criminal justice systems. We have seen that even within one country there have been changes in recorded crime depending on legal changes and to alterations in the method of recording. Between countries there are also differences in the point at which the crime is measured. For some it does not occur until the suspect is found and the papers forwarded to the prosecutor. There are also differences according to data quality and to the overall list of offenses included in the overall crime figures. Because of these factors it might seem prudent to avoid some overall comparisons. However, one possibility is to look at changes in the crime rate taking into account the assumption that the main factors have remained constant.

Refer Table 2.12

The table shows that of all the countries listed England and Wales had the greatest increase in crime at 44%. The next highest were Belgium and Portugal (32%) followed by Austria and Italy at 28%.

Refer Table 2.13

The results show that the European prison population for these sixteen countries increased from 238,000 in 1987 to 279,000 in 1993 which is an increase of 11.7 per cent. So there has clearly been an overall movement towards the greater use of imprisonment in recent years. Northern Ireland was the European country with the highest proportion of the population in prison and Southern Ireland had the lowest proportion. People in the north were twice as likely to be in prison as those in the south. Scotland had the second highest proportion of people in prison and Portugal was third. England and Wales was fifth, behind Italy third and Austria fourth. Since 1993 the prison population in England and Wales has risen from 46,633 to 51,086 in June 1995 and to 52,731 in early December 1995 and 53,974 in April 1996 (Travis 1996 p4, 1996 p2).

The overall figures mask wide variations in experience between countries. The number of people in prison in Greece and Holland has been rising rapidly and increased by 64% and 61% respectively between 1987 and 1993. Four other countries have also had substantial increases in the number of prisoners over the six year period. These were Italy with a 46% rise, Sweden 38%, Norway 35% and Portugal 32%. Only one country had more than a marginal reduction in prison population and this was Finland with a fall of 18% over the six year period (Home Office 1994 p24).

<u>Why the prison populations changed.</u> The large increases in the six countries may in part may reflect the fact that politicians have been promising their population to get 'tough on crime'. It may also because of the increase in the number of more serious crimes. It is therefore instructive to tabulate the changes in violent crime and domestic burglary with the changes in size of prison population.

Refer Table 2.14

The table above gives figures on the change in prison population related to changes in crimes known to the police and the level of violent crime. These are for the home countries and European ones with large swings in prison population. It might be expected that countries with the increasing rates of crime would be the ones with the increasing prison populations. However, considered in this light the figures show a distinct lack of logic. The three countries with the largest increases in prison population were Greece, the Netherlands and Italy. However, they both had a smaller increase in their crime rates than both Finland and England and Wales which were the countries with declining prison populations over the period. The fact that the prison population in England and Wales declined slightly between 1987-93 might at first seem surprising as it occurred against the backdrop of a 42% increase in all crimes recorded by the police, over a 50 per cent increase in violent crime and nearly a fifty per cent increase in domestic burglary (Home Office 1994 p23).

Since 1993 there has been a slight fall in crime in England and Wales. This might have been expected to lead to a decline in the prison population. However it has risen and in fact by July 1995 was 51,100 which is a twelve per cent increase. These kind of facts show the lack of correlation between the level of crime and the prison population.

Conclusion These figures overall show up the increase in crime, with the latest figures available showing the more serious ones being at the highest ever level. The data also shows the lack of logic in the international trends with countries increasing or decreasing their prison population based presumably upon political considerations rather than on the number of crimes.

Delinquency

Chapter 3

In this chapter some of the major theories of delinquency are introduced.

Early academic approaches to crime

Sir Cyril Burt first published his study <u>The Young Delinquent</u> in 1925 and he said that 37,520 persons were charged in juvenile courts in 1913. Almost exactly 20,000 were under age of 14 and 2,000 were female (1944 ed p44). These numbers rose during the war to 51,323 in 1917 and Burt thought that the family was a factor in leading to crime;

'The ordinary child in an ordinary home is the member of a small and self contained society, cared for by the united effort of both father and mother, and possessing at least one other relative of his own age and outlook to play with him (1944 p95)'.

He believed there was a failure to provide a good family life for an increasing number of children and this could lead to them committing crime. In part the inadequate family life was due to the overcrowding amongst the poor which he defined as a home with 2 or more adults per room. In this definition two children under ten counted as one adult. He found that 21% delinquents compared to only 16% of non delinquents of the same social strata live in such overcrowded conditions and that in the country as a whole it was 11 per cent (1944 p87).

Another factor was a too early acquaintance with sex and in

39

this respect he commented that with poor people *'premature acquaintance with conjugal relations is all but unavoidable'*. He also felt that family breakdown was a factor. In this respect he commented about children being raised by surrogate families:

Inquiring into case after case, the investigator cannot fail to be struck with the marked recurrence of one suggestive item- the presence of foster-parents (1944 p93).

He also said that the war had led to the *'controlling hand of a father or elder brother'* being removed. The mother often had to work and *'would be absent throughout the very hours when the child needed her vigilance at home'* (1944 p94). He continued to state that due to the dislocation due to the war many children were separated from their parents for a large proportion of their early life. This led to them being unsettled and for there to be less chance of self discipline or a code of right behaviour to be formed (1944 p94). He noted that misconduct is nearly twice as common with children born out of wedlock as with children born within it. This he felt was possibly due to the lack of a father figure. He also said that often the delinquent was the only child of the family (1944 94n).

He proposed that defective discipline might be leading to delinquency. Parents may be too lenient, strict or non existent. In some families the child may be cajoled one minute and whipped the next. In a phrase that was in later years to be (nearly) reinvented by right wing politicians he stated: *The shock of a sharp, short separation will often rouse the casual offender to his senses (1944 p107).'*

However, Burt did not regard the family itself as the main cause of delinquency. He maintained that children found the homes overbearing and there was nothing at home for the children to play with and so they go out. He maintained that it was once outside the home the influences leading to delinquency were found. These were unemployment, alienation from school or work, the bad influence of some adults but above all the influence of others his own age (1944 p186).

Sheldon and Eleanor Glueck These two placed more blame on the family and promoted the idea that bad families produce bad children (Wilson and Herrstein 1985 p215). They conducted a ten year study of delinquent boys in the Boston area which was published in 1950. This maintained that if certain factors were held constant such as age, race, neighbourhood and intelligence then delinquency appeared to be due to a combination of some personal factors. An additional cause of crime was a family background in which the parents were indifferent or hostile to the child and erratic in disciplinary practices. This research had certain methodological problems, however. The investigators knew, for example, whether the boy was delinquent or not when they assessed the family and so their views could therefore easily have been coloured.

Psychological explanations of crime

In his book Forty four Juvenile Thieves Bowlby argued that boys who had become attached to their mother but then separated from her were more likely to steal than those who had no such separation. Objects might be seen as 'love objects'. Bowlby expressed great importance to maternal bonding which he saw as maternal love, with a warm intimate relationship and continuous caring. The absence of this he saw as 'maternal deprivation' and where it occurred he saw many physiological and behaviourial problems including delinquency. There are of course great problems with Bowlby's interpretation with there being, for example, questions as to the father's role or whether a group of close relatives could not supply the support for a child's needs.

In his critique of Bowlby, Michael Rutter distinguished between those children who had a relationship and had it disrupted and those children who did not develop one in the first place. Rutter suggested that if the bond is formed a period of separation can be overcome. However:

'If the bond never forms, the consequences can be very severe. Rutter suggests that the absence of attachment may lead to "affectionless psychopathy," which he describes as beginning with "an initial phase of clinging, dependent behaviour, followed by attention seeking, uninhibited, indiscriminate friendliness and finally a personality characterised by the lack of guilt, an inability to keep rules and an inability to form lasting relationships (Wilson and Herrstein 1985 p223).

For many people crime is a transitory phenomena which teenagers become involved with during their youth, possibly as part of delinquent subcultures and then move out of as they mature. There have been wide differences in youth culture between Britain and the United States. One of the large differences noted by Downes in the 1960s was the absence of gangs in Britain (1965 p116).

Positivism <u>Matza</u> in his classic book
Delinquency and Drift (1964) argued that in the previous

hundred years positivist criminology was in the ascendency. This approach he maintained had three fundamental assumptions (p3).

a) The concentration on the individual criminal rather than the criminal law as the main point of departure. So according to this view the main explanation of crime is located 'in the motivational and behaviourial systems of criminals' (p3). He continued to point out that criminology had changed from emphasising biological factors. In the nineteenth century Lombroso had emphasised the shapes of the heads of criminals but this had change to the emphasis on more sophisticated psychological and sociological explanations. However, the fundamental fact is that the focus is on the offender and not the crime.

b) The positive school has a quest for scientific status. He maintained that, whereas the classic school argued the doctrine of 'free will' as underlying crime, the positivist stressed their scientific determinism and rejected the idea of free will. Matza maintains that to the positivist *Every event is caused. Human freedom is illusory' (1964 p5).* He did, however, continue to distinguish between 'hard' and 'soft' determinism aand maintained that instead of the polarity people are both free and constrained.

c) He said the positivsts feel the delinquent is fundamentally different from the non delinquent. Because of this assumption each of the positivist theorists has tried to accentuate the difference between criminals and non criminals.

According to Matza the positivist propose:

'Delinquency results from an aggressive or antisocial

personality arising out of parental neglect, or perhaps over indulgence, or perhaps inconsistency; from a delinquent self image arising out of criminal or delinquent role models, or perhaps an. overbearing maternal figure who for reasons of her own encourages or too vehemently opposes antisocial behaviour .. (or) an inability to fathom the realistic consequences of transgression and an incapacity to resist the lure of companions (1964 p17).

A) Sociological theories

a) <u>Anomie theories</u>. I mentioned Durkheim in the introduction but the most complete theorist in this area is Robert Merton. He noted that the poorest groups had the highest rate of crime as measured by official statistics. These groups suffered anomie because they were taught that there was equality of opportunity. The fact that it did not exist led to dissatisfaction and possibly criminality.

<u>Merton</u> argued that industrial societies effectively blocked access to success for parts of the population. The society makes it wrong to achieve successes by means which are not sanctioned by the legal institutions of the society. So common success goals and closed access to achieving these leads to deviant behaviour on a large scale (1957 ch 4 and 5).

Merton identified four kinds of non conformity derived from the differential acceptance of means and ends. In developed societies great emphasis is placed upon the achievement of success in material terms which helps create the motivation in society. However, it presents problems to those hampered in terms of achieving success such as the ethnic minorities or children of the working class. Overall Merton identified five kinds of adaption to society as follows:

44

<u>Conformity</u> This is where people have the goals of the society and also obey the rules in order to follow them. He did, however, note that sometimes conformity can be foolhardy.

<u>Innovation</u> This involves the search for new means in addition to those already accepted or proscribed by the culture. Some of these may be condemned by the society. Fraud and robbery would come into this category. However, other activities may be simply frowned upon such as institutionalised gambling. The situation where there is a lack of agreement on socially recognised means was viewed by Durkheim as an important factor leading to social disintegration. He called it 'anomie' and said it was due to rapid social change. However, if the social pressure was so strong that this did not occur then change and innovation would be inhibited. As we have seen it is for this reason he saw crime in society as 'normal'.

<u>Ritualism</u> This involves giving up the pursuit of ends and pursuing security in the ritualistic involvement in means. Sometimes the rules involved in petty bureaucracy can make the perpetrators feel secure.

<u>Retreatism</u> This reaction involves the abandonment of both the goals and the sanctioned patterns of behaviour. These people retreat from the involvement in life towards the role of the fatalistic and passive onlooker.

<u>Rebellion</u> This is the total rejection of both culturally approved ends and means. This could be the political rejection of the dominant values of society such as in the French Revolution. Furthermore people such as beatniks or

hippies reject material ends for achieved values such as creative experiences.

We can tabulate Merton's suggestions according to values and means.

Types of conformity and non conformity

	Values (ends)	norms (approved means)
1 Conformity	+	+
2 Innovation	+	-
3 Ritualism	-	+
4 Retreatism	+	+
	-	-
5 Rebellion	-	-

B) Subcultural theories

These explanations stress the importance of the social situation rather than the role of the individual. However, it is clear that sociologists have been influenced by the ideas of the positivists and for this reason concentrated on the differences between the delinquent and 'normal' teenagers. Matza rightly criticised this approach and argued that if delinquents were that different then delinquency would not be such a transient thing. He said Delinquents are only so intermittently- a delinquent is so because the shoe fits but he does not wear it for much of the time (1964 p26).

An important development in criminological theory occurred in 1955 when Albert Cohen published 'Delinquent Boys'. In this he first employed the term 'subculture' in relation to certain forms of juvenile delinquency. To Cohen a subculture was a 'culture within a culture.'

David Downes developed this idea and suggested that the subcultures should be divided up into:

a) Those that form *outside* the dominant culture such as the culture of immigrant groups or regional cultures which become merged with the dominant culture.

b) Those which form *within* the context of the dominant culture.

Downes proposed these could be of two kinds. They can either be negative towards it such as delinquent subcultures, messianic groups, or political extremist subcultures. However, they may be positive towards it as would be the case with occupational subcultures. In fact we can see that there are a whole range of subcultures very positive towards the dominant culture.

Miller

His theory is that delinquency in poorer areas is not in opposition to the dominant culture. Rather it is the direct intensified expression of the dominant culture pattern of the lower class community. This would be a long established culture pattern with an integrity of its own.

Miller, identified lower class culture as having a female based household whose main feature is a lack of reliance on an adult male. It also has six focal concerns which may be placed against alternatives as follows:

Area		alternatives
Trouble	A desire to avoid this but admiration of those who have wild behaviour	refusal to risk trouble for excitement.
Toughness	physical prowess, skill; masculinity, fearlessness even if illegal,	weakness, effeminacy, timidity, ineptitude cowardice, caution.
Smartness	ability to outsmart, making money by wits, shrewdness, adroitness in repartee.	gullibility making money by hard work, dull wittedness, verbal maladroitness, slowness
Excitement	thrill, danger, risk; change, activity.	boredom, 'deadness', safeness, sameness, passivity.

Fate	being lucky, favoured by 'fortune'.	being unlucky, ill omened.
Autonomy	independence, freedom,	dependency, 'being cared for', presence of external constraint and strong authority.

So to Miller the working class youth had one set of values and the conformist middle class system a totally different set. This theory is in some senses at the opposite end of the spectrum to Merton who stressed the similarity of values.

Matza and Sykes produced a theory of delinquency which Matza extended in his book **Delinquency and Drift**. In their article they proposed that in a society there are conventional values and running alongside these are *subterranean* values. So they wrote that *'the search for adventure, excitement and thrill is a subterranean value...that often exists side by side with the values of security, routinisation and the rest. It is not a deviant value, in any full sense, but must be held in abeyance until the proper moment and circumstances for its expression arrive (1957 p 71).*

In this light a delinquent is not a person with totally different values but perhaps one who accentuates the subterranean values against the more formal ones. In **The Drugtakers** Jock Young clearly set out the differences between the two sets of values (1971 p126):

Formal and subterranean Values

Formal Work Values	Subterranean values
1 Deferred gratification	short term hedonism
2 Planning future action	spontaneity
3 Conformity to bureaucracy	ego-expressivity
4 High control over detail little over direction	autonomy, control over behaviour in detail and direction.
5 Routine, predictability	new experience, excitement
6 Instrumental attitudes to work	activities performed as an end in themselves.
7 hard productive work seen as a virtue	disdain for work.

The subterranean values are in many respects similar to the working class 'focal concerns set out by Miller. For other people the difference between the two sets of values may well be the difference between work and leisure. People work hard and then in their social life enjoy spontaneous activities.

Matza saw delinquents as drifting between the two sets of values and generally leaning too far towards the subterranean values. However, he suggested that the novice practitioner is often surprised at how like other children the delinquent can be at times. He continued:

The image of the delinquent I wish to convey is one of drift; an actor neither compelled nor committed to deeds nor freely choosing them; neither different in any simple or fundamental sense from the law abiding, nor the same; conforming to certain traditions in American life while partially unreceptive to other more conventional traditions.......Drift stands midway between freedom and control. Its basis is an area of the social structure in which control has been loosened, couple with the abortiveness of adolescent endeavour to organise an autonomous subculture and thus an independent source of control around illegal action. The delinquent transiently exists in a limbo between convention and crime, responding in turn to the demands of each, flirting now with one, now with the other, but postponing commitment, evading decision. Thus, he drifts between criminal and conventional action (p28).'

So Matza does not regard the delinquents as being committed to criminal lifestyles. On some occasions they may succumb to temptation but most of the time they will probably not be engaged in such activity.

Schur Radical non intervention. In a section on public attitudes towards crime he asserts that there is an inordinate focus on the individual offenders themselves rather than on the social processes involved in crime. He said the general public regards delinquents as being basically different from non offenders quite apart from the mere differences in engaging in norm violations. They take a view close to that of the positivists which is that it is in the basic difference that the causes of delinquency lie. He commented:

Delinquent acts have usually been viewed as symptomatic of an underlying disorder. Sometimes that disorder has been seen to lie in the individual himself, at other times in the social system. In either case, this notion has an important implication for research and policy; namely that one must understand and treat the underlying condition and not merely its symptoms' (Schur 1973 p31).

He gave as an example of this approach research reported in

the NYT which suggested that experts had discovered a learning problem which may have affected 80% of delinquents and led to their problems. These *'may have begun their downhill ride in society with a potentially correctable learning problem'*. Schur also suggested that there is no convincing evidence that 'broken homes' led to delinquency and set out contrasting reactions to deviancy amongst liberal reformers and radical non interventionists as follows (1973 p44):

Liberal Reform	Radical non intervention

Basic assumptions

delinquency concentrated in the lower class	Delinquency widespread throughout society
individual constrained particularly	basic role of
contingencies	neo anti-determinism
by subcultural pressures	
social determinism	

Favoured methodologies

Analysis of rate variations	Self reports;
ecological anaylysis	observation;
study of subcultures	legal analysis

Focal point for research

Social class	Interaction between the
Local community	individual and the legal *System*

Representative causal perspectives

Anomie theories	labelling analysis;
cultural transmission	drift
opportunity theory	and situational theories.

Prevention

Street gang work	De-emphasis on singling
community programmes	out specific individuals
piecemeal socio-economic reform	radical socio-cultural changes.

Treatment

Community programmes	Voluntary treatment
improving conditions in institutions	

Juvenile Court

Better training and caseloads	Narrow scope of
more attention to social factors	juvenile court jurisdiction; increased formalisation.

Schur relied a great deal on the interactionist or labelling perspective and made suggestions for radical non intervention.

* We must get rid of the idea that the delinquent is basically different (p153).

* *'Most types of youthful misconduct are common within all socioeconomic strata in our society'.*

* *'The kinds of causal variables that traditionally have dominated research provide only limited understanding of delinquency problems'.*

* So-called delinquents are not much different from non delinquents except when they have been processed by the courts.

* *'The primary target for delinquency policy should be neither the individual not the local community setting, but rather the delinquency defining processes themselves (p154).'*

* This does not mean that anything goes, or that all behaviour is socially acceptable. But traditional delinquency policy has proscribed youthful behaviour well beyond what is required to maintain a smooth running society.

* 'The basic injunction for public policy becomes: *Leave well alone*
wherever possible.'

British developments

Parkhurst Prison for boys was opened in 1838 as a response to the 'moral panic' about juvenile gangs. The first secure institution designed specifically for juveniles was set up in Borstal in Kent following the Prevention of Crime act 1908 (McClintock 1995 p1037). In 1933 there was a change in philosophy with the Children's and Young Person's Act. It directed the magistrates to take account first of the child's welfare and individual needs rather than to fully enforce the sentence that would be imposed for a responsible adult. In 1964 the Longford report stated that delinquents were a product of their society and a reflection of its failure to socialise children properly. Following this report the Children and Young Person's Act 1969, was held as the century's most overt policy of decriminalisation. It allowed care proceedings as an alternative for all children aged 10-14 years. However, despite this attempt the number of juveniles sent to detention centres rose by 225% between 1971 and 1977.

In 1991 the Criminal Justice Act introduced new powers for the courts to impose a 'secure training order' which allowed those aged 12-14 to be detained in secure surroundings. The first aim was for private funds to build the new institutions. However, the courts have detained more juveniles than there are places and consequently many 15 and 16 year old boys are detained in adult prisons. From the year October 1993 to October 1994 the number of boys detained in prison rose by 86% (McClintock 1995).

The evidence shows that the prisons do not make rehabilitation a primary concern and even constructive regimes have high reconviction rates. The Dartington Social Research Unit found a 76% reconviction rate. Carson and Martel found that 78% of their sample re-offended within a year and 40% had committed six or more offenses. (Milham, Bullock and Hosie 1978, Carson and Martell 1979). Commenting on these findings McClintock states:

These researchers concluded that admission to such units increased the probability of re-offending, especially in younger children; and by comparison with previous records they also concluded that admission to such a unit increased the likelihood of further crimes. Later studies produced no evidence to change this view (1995 p1038).

There is evidence that the Government recognises the high reconviction rates and the 1988 Green Paper Punishment, Custody and the Community made it clear that *'even a short period of custody is likely to confirm them as criminals, particularly as they acquire new criminal skills from more sophisticated offenders.'*

Another problem is that secure units are spread around the country and consequently young offenders are often long distances from their families. This makes it harder to maintain their support networks and problems such as bullying can lead to suicides.

McClintock said that, although it may be politically attractive to be tough on crime, it does not work. He called for the funds to be diverted from expensive building programmes into community measures (1995).

Terrence Morris (1957) stated that a working class child is adequately socialised but into a 'subculture unambiguously defined and in some respects blatantly at variance with widely accepted middle class norms'. In this sense he was approaching the kind of analysis put forward by Miller in the USA.

Derek Allcorn wrote an important, but hitherto unpublished Manchester University Ph D analysis of British youth culture in the 1950s. He stressed the class nature:

'Social class is a most important factor in the social development of young people and an examination of the connections between social class and social development must constitute an important part of any study of the latter'

He continued to show the difference between middle class and working class youth on a variety of factors. For example, the working class youths had a well developed street culture in their locality in contrast to the more 'privatised' existence of the middle classes. He commented:

The role of 'keeping yourself to yourself' was strictly observed by adults and extended by them to their children. I rarely saw children playing in the streets in these districts.

He also stressed the fact that middle class teenagers were more likely to be connected with formal associations whereas the working class were involved with informal organised activities and 'commercial recreations'. Working class boys had much higher attendance at variety shows and the cinema and furthermore began attending dances at an earlier age. He further suggested that working class boys started talking to girls and playing games with them about the age of 14, whereas middle class lads started two years later.

He found that peer groups generally developed from children's play groups. Among the young children the groups would contain both sexes but as the boys grew older they spent more time in games of football and 'fighting' which led to greater segregation. Furthermore, the girls were normally constrained to help in the home and possibly in looking after the younger children. So from about the age of ten the groups were segregated by sex.

The peer group increased in activity until the ages 16-18 when almost all the young men in the area of study preferred to spend their leisure time with a peer group going out at least five times a week with Saturday night being almost sacred. The relationships in the group were anti-authoritarian and leaderless in that, although one person might be the leader in one activity, in an alternative situation it would fall upon another. They tended to 'treat' other members in the group and to spend to the limits of their income. The culture of the group was one of immediate gratification and was opposed to the development of romantic relationships. Allcorn commented:

When one of them was going out with a girl, the others subjected them to a continuous stream of satirical and bawdy comments. (A relationship) was something that happened to them, and in which they played little or no active part' (p271).

This research in the fifties is congruent with Jephcott's findings about the thirties and early forties. My studies of peer groups in the 1970's also found that little had changed during the intervening twenty years (Francome 1976 chapter four). Allcorn argued that a key factor in the breakup of peer groups was the substitution of the network of relationships with peers by a serious relationship with a girl leading to marriage.

Their ultimate fate was sealed. Peer groups and gangs alike broke up when their members formed stable relationships with girls...The organisation of both included a principle which ensured their eventual disintegration- the exclusion of girls (Allcorn 1955 p262).

To these and the groups I studied in Swindon the law was something that was broken if it were convenient to do so. The teenagers would have no compunction about going into a movie or a pub under age. There were a variety of situations where physical assault would be required, for example, if someone insulted your mother. There would also be no compunction about receiving some stolen goods. However, there was no consistent law breaking. So Matza's comment about the shoe not fitting too often was apt for this group.

Jock Young (1971) said the apparent social disorganisation of slum areas is often merely organisation centring around values different than those of respectable society. What is perceived as the as the faulty childbearing practices of individual families is more easily understood as differential socialisation occurring in different groups and utilising different techniques.

Stan Cohen in his book **Folk Devils and Moral Panics** (1971) considered society's reaction to the mods and rockers. He proposed that these forms of youth subculture were more a creation of the media than a reaction of working class youth to their economic and social environment. The press built up a few minor incidents which occurred at Easter in 1964 using words like 'riot' and 'battle'. The newspapers predicted that riots would happen again and it became a self fulfilling prophecy as young people began to go to where they thought the action would be.

Cohen argued that a problem for newspapers was that if there was very little news to report to make the papers interesting it may be seen necessary to create it. They took the side of the establishment-the police, magistrates and local people against the youth and so were able to use the youth as a scapegoat.

David Downes in his book **The Delinquent Solution** drew attention to Turner's distinction between the education system in Britain being characterised by 'sponsored mobility' and the

United States being characterised by 'contest mobility'. Under the British system the idea was to choose those being selected for elite positions as early as possible. In the United States the contest was left open as long as possible. Downes was critical of the education system which did not engage the working class youth and their realisation that they would only obtain 'dead end' jobs. He noted that with automation even these jobs might not be available and could result in deviancy of explosive proportions. So he called for education to be made much more attractive for these young men.

He also advocated an extension of the youth service to make it attractive to the young people who would otherwise go out 'on the town.'

Willis followed Downes in stressing the importance of the education system in his book **Learning to Labour**. He stated that for the working class youth the education system was a process which condemned them to jobs at the lower end of the social scale. They saw the education system as largely irrelevant to their position and could well reject it.

Tom McClintock, a psychiatrist, wrote on article on creating new criminals for the BMJ (Oct 1995) in response to the new 'get tough' approach to violent and persistent criminals put forward at the Conservative Party Conference. He maitained that the argument that teenage behaviour was a threat to society has been continuous one for over a hundred and fifty years. However, in the 1980s considerable expertise was developed in the UK for community based programmes for young offenders. As a result there was a 75% drop in the number of juveniles receiving custodial sentences. There was, however, a U turn in Government policy and increased use of imprisonment for the young. This was a development he regretted.

Discussion There has been some evidence of gangs in Britain and James Patrick's book **A Glasgow Gang Observed** is a case in point. However, generally British groups formed themselves into peer groups which were based more on equality. This is a continuing major difference between Britain and the United States.

Young people in all developed societies have higher than average crime rates compared to the older age groups. In part this may be due simply to age. Thus, young people may be charged with under age purchase of cigarettes or alcohol or under age sex. However, young men in particular also tend to belong to peer groups or gangs and these can lead them into committing offenses. So in a conflict situation the young man would be expected to stand and fight with his friends, he might also be expected to commit perjury to help a 'mate' keep out of trouble. This kind of crime is, however, of temporary duration as the peer groups diminish in importance with age.

On the whole the criminological theorists have made important contributions to our understanding of youth and crime. Some of the theorisation on subcultural development will also be important when we come to discuss terrorism.

Chapter 4

Right wing and Crime

Four years into office in 1983 an interviewer said to Mrs Thatcher that she was reported to be in favour of Victorian values'. She answered: *'Oh exactly. Very much so. Those were the values when our country became great'* (Himmelfarb 1995 p3). There were also others in the Conservative administration who called for a return to Victorian values. This call may be seen as a reversion to a time when there was certainty over what was correct behaviour. Those who wish for a return to Victorian values see it as a time when people knew the difference between 'right and wrong'. Crime was due to some individuals choosing the wrong path. The modern right wing tends to share certain beliefs as follows:

1 Most people in society keep the law and recognise that it is just.

2 Private property is very important and needs to be protected.

3 There are a small number of people who through greed, lust or for other reasons break the laws of society. They need to be caught and punished so that society is protected from them and they learn the error of their ways.

Let us further consider the right wing view of crime in terms of the focal points discussed in chapter one.

A) Attitude to major social institutions.

The right wing have generally been positive towards the dominant institutions especially those with the support of the middle classes. There was a time where the Church of England was called the 'Conservative Party at prayer'. However, the 'new right' has been more critical, especially where the institutions have had Government financial support and so are reputed to have caused higher taxes. These it feels have a tendency to grow and increase the amount of support they receive from the state without necessarily producing any comparative benefit.

B) Attitude to the family.

Those from the right have stressed the role of the family in preventing crime and conversely single parenthood as a potential cause of it.

In her autobiography 'The Downing Street Years', Margaret Thatcher argued that the increase in crime during her administration could not be due to poverty because the number of offenses has risen both in times of prosperity and recession. She thought it was rooted in the home life and the need to strengthen the traditional family. She continued to say:

Of course family breakdown and single parenthood did not mean that juvenile delinquency would inevitably follow: grandparents, friends and neighbours can in some circumstances help lone mothers to cope quite well. But all the evidence -statistical and anecdotal- pointed to the breakdown of families as the starting point for a range of social ills of which getting into trouble with the police was only one. Boys who lack the guidance of a father are more likely to suffer social problems of all kinds. (Thatcher 1995 p629).

She also stated that teenage pregnancy might be due to the state benefit system.

'Young girls were tempted to become pregnant because that brought them a council flat and an income from the state'(Thatcher 1995 p629).

However, under the Conservative administration that took office in 1979 the changes in the family were by no means towards a

Victorian style of family.

Norman Dennis His theory in a nutshell is that two things have happened since the Second World War. The first is that there has been a breakdown in the family and secondly that as a result of family breakdown there has been a large increase in crime.

He argued rightly that after the second world war many people expected crime rates to fall and they felt that crime was generally rare. He noted the fact that George Orwell stated in 1944:

An imaginary foreign observer would certainly be struck by our gentleness; by the orderly behaviour of English crowds, the lack of pushing and quarrelling...And except for certain well-defined areas in half a dozen big towns, there is very little crime or violence. (Dennis p15)

Dennis also quoted Gorer's comments published in 1955:

The English are certainly among the most peaceful, gentle, courteous and orderly populations that the civilised world has seen...the control of aggression has gone to such remarkable lengths that you hardly ever see a fight in a bar (a not uncommon spectacle in most of the rest of Europe or the USA), (and) football crowds are as orderly as church meetings (1955 p16)

A third quotation was from K B Smellie, a professor at the LSE, in 1955

'There can be little doubt that the life of towns has steadily improved..Drunkenness has fallen steadily. So too has public violence...From the Yahoo habits of eighteenth century London we have passed into a ...rationality of ordered processions and patient queues. And, almost certainly with the passing of violence, drunkenness and squalor, has gone much cruelty as well. Personal relations are more gentle and, as one observer has said, 'the

contemporary English would appear to have as unaggressive a public life as any recorded people'(Smellie 1955 p24).

So Dennis argued that crime remained at relatively low levels until 1955 when it was just above 1000 crimes per 100,000 population.

He also reports a review of family life in 1956 by GDH Cole who said it was the basic social unit. He stated that it had improved, that quarrelling was less common due to improved housing and there had been a notable improvement in the care of children. There were better opportunities for games than in previous generations and the proportion of children neglected had declined (Dennis 1993 p35).

However, Dennis argued crime then began a great rise to 1700 per 100,000 population by 1960. Then from 1960 the rate of increase was of a much higher order than had hitherto existed. It rose to 2700 per 100,000 in 1965. He suggested that at this time:

The usual explanation was that people were less likely to behave themselves well when the money in their pockets removed the requirement that they must live their lives prudently. Low unemployment was particularly to blame for the rise in the crime rate. Why should a young man worry about his reputation, or even his criminal record, when he could walk with ease from one job to another (1993 p1).

Dennis stated that in the 1950s and 1960s it was widely accepted that a young man in trouble with the law who was from a broken home (ie without a father) was automatically entitled to the court's sympathy. The growth in the crime rate was partly attributed to the failure of family supervision and the growth in number of 'latch key' children (1993 p2).

Dennis contested that in recent years there have been great changes in the activities of conceiving and the bringing up of children. In the past behaviour was closely monitored. According to him:

The intention was to ensure that, as far as possible before a man had sexual intercourse with a woman, he should undertake far reaching, long lasting and wide ranging commitments to his possible child and the mother of his possible child'(Dennis 1993 p3)

He suggested that there had been three changes which have reduced a man's link to his children. These are first an increase in the divorce rate. So, while only 1 in 80 marriages ended in divorce before their sixth anniversary in 1951, in 1981 it was one in nine (1993 p5). Secondly an increase in co-habiting. This meant the man was less likely to have to make a binding commitment. He could have sexual intercourse without public censure and without the life-long commitment that a traditional marriage would normally bring. He argued that the evidence showed that people who have had 'trial marriages' are more likely to get divorced than those that have not. Thirdly there had been a reduction in the degree of certainty that a father would be looking after his children.

He produced figures on the increase in illegitimacy. In 1961 6 per cent of all births occurred *'without the man having publicly committed himself to the child through marriage'*. In 1971 it was 8 per cent, in 1981 it was 13 per cent but by 1991 in was over 30 per cent. Lone mothers were the fastest growing group. He continued to say that the separation of impregnation from pregnancy allows men to escape the consequences of fatherhood. He maintained that it is always the case that men can escape the consequences of parenthood more easily than women. However:

What is new is that the whole project of creating and maintaining the skills and duties and motivations of fatherhood and of imposing on men duties towards their own children that are as difficult as possible to escape, is being abandoned...Young men with a short

66

term view of life and hedonistic values have looked on with quiet delight, scarcely able to believe their luck (Dennis 1993 p7).

So a basic problem for Dennis is that the social definition of what it is to be a man has changed. He further maintained that the intelligentsia has been in support (1993 p9). Dennis was very critical of Marxism, which he said gave a primacy to the influence of material factors on peoples lives. In this respect he quoted Marx's well known comment on the way that material conditions affect the way people perceive the world;

It is not the consciousness of men that determines their being, but, on the contrary, their social being that determines their consciousness'(Dennis 1993 p15).

He continued to say that this doctrine had now reached some of the most conservative parts of the society including the Church of England with the proposition that crime is caused by poverty, bad housing and unemployment. He stated that one modern version of Marxism as applied to family life is that economic factors are dominant in explaining its change. The early industrial economy needed child labour and mobile expendable young males so big flexible households resulted:

The maturing industrial economy 'required' a steadier 'well drilled proletariat. Therefore women and children were ushered out of the labour force and husbands 'employed' wives at the kitchen sink. Contemporary capitalism creates jobs for women 'because they are cheaper and more tractable' (Dennis 1993 p15).

He continued to say that Marxists believe that the shift from the disorderly working class of 1800 to the sober, respectable working class of 1950 was essentially a result of economic change. Furthermore he maintained they believe that the shift to the father absent family is also a result of economic change.

Dennis argued that the intelligentsia dismissed the figures of rising crime with scorn. He quoted Patricia Morgan in support of this view and commented;

The increase in crime was a statistical mirage that misled only simpletons. The enlightened response to the popular consensus was to mock it as a 'moral panic'; the public was not responding to a growth in criminal conduct, it was reacting to 'images of deviance' (1973 p25).

The bibliography makes it clear that what he was criticising here were two of Stan Cohen's books '**Folk Devils and Moral Panics**' and the '**Images of Deviance**' and also the book Cohen wrote with Jock Young '**The manufacture of news: Deviance, social problems and the mass media** (1973).' Of course in later works, probably not known to Dennis, Young was quite clear that the crime rates had increased and specifically attacked the position of the far left on this issue.

Dennis continued to argue that some within the intelligentsia have seen the rise in crime as a sensible protest against society.

It is thus clear and admirable that new generations have emerged who have realised that the old ways were 'a confidence trick played on the poor and disadvantaged'. To these newer generations litter dropping is, commendably not a 'lapse in social behaviour to be 'corrected' but (presumably) an heroic act of defiance (1993 p27).

He continued to say that many societies in the past have made the law breaker the hero. However, in the past the encouragement was for lawlessness against tyrannous regimes abroad. What is new is the suggestion that lawlessness should be exonerated when used on behalf of the *relatively deprived* at home. He was also critical of such books as the New Criminology because in its view:

The deviant is no longer the proper object of society's control. She or he is the society's saviour. In the 1970s and into the 1980s, the superiority of the world-view of the criminal over that of the law abiding citizen became the stock in trade of the dominant New Criminology and Critical Sociology (1993 p31).

This kind of comment shows that Dennis did not understand the main thrust of the argument of the New Criminologists who were not defending criminal actions. Rather, what they were saying was that if we set up a different kind of society which is not concerned with acquisition of property then we will be not be producing people who will become thieves. For example, they argued that 96% of crimes were crimes against property and so its abolition would remove the basis for the vast majority of crimes.

Another part of the argument from Dennis is that the intellectuals have stated that the family is not in decline but is simply changing. In this sense Dennis believes they have not realised the danger to society by the decline in the family. His book contains a whole chapter entitled 'Not deteriorating only changing'. However he argued that more recently people have begun to realise that this position is untenable.

Patricia Morgan

The right wing sociologist Patricia Morgan takes a similar position to Dennis in her book <u>Farewell to the Family</u>. She argues marriage acts as a barrier to crime. In her view it is the *'most successful corrective institution ever devised as so many criminological investigations into recidivism will testify* (1995 p144). She continued to say that marriage also was a factor why so many juvenile delinquents did stop misbehaving or in David Matza's tern 'drifted out of delinquency. She quoted Matza:

Boys are less driven to prove manhood unconventionally through deeds or misdeeds when with the passing of time they may effortlessly exhibit the conventional signposts of manhood-physical appearance, the completion of school, job, marriage, and perhaps even children' (Matza 1964 p55).

Marriage then helps men to mature. In addition Morgan believes there is a second way that the family prevents delinquency. This is because having a good family name can be important and so teenagers would not wish to cause trouble and ruin the reputation of their family.

To Morgan the reasons for the increase in crime since the nineteen fifties are linked to poor socialisation. One argument is that parents do not teach children the difference between 'right and wrong'. This poor socialisation according to Patricia Morgan leads to:

The spread of what could be called the delinquent syndrome, a conglomeration of behaviour, speech, appearance and attitudes, a frightening ugliness and hostility which pervades human interaction, a flaunting of contempt for other human beings, a delight in crudity, cruelty and violence, a desire to challenge and humiliate, and never, but never, to please (Morgan 1978 p13).

A third part of the attitude to crime of the right wing is that it is due in large part to the actions of immigrants.

Hypermasculine males

We have seen that one family factor relevant to the right is the rise in single parenthood. It maintains that this leads to many young men not being brought up with good male role models. Some theorists have proposed that boys who are brought up in female dominated households may become 'hypermasculine'. The argument is that such boys attempt to overcome their female identification and overcompensate by performing aggressive acts which may well be targeted against women.

70

They quote a study of delinquents at an Ohio boy's school where it was concluded that boys from 'mother based' households exhibited the following characteristics:

1 They over emphasised their manliness and toughness.

2 They emphasised themselves as sexual athletes and pursued women as sexual objects.

3 They were more impulsive and hostile than other boys.

4 They were more likely to bow to the pressure of the peer group.

5 they were more likely to take part in high risk behaviour for thrills.

In all the researchers believed that in order to compensate for being brought up in a female dominated situation they came to regard anti-social and aggressive behaviour as a means to promote the image of a real man (Silverman and Dinitz 1974, Scully 1990 p66). In response to such comments Scully discussed the relevance of such considerations to rape and commented:

The problem with these theories is that they dwell on the 'unfitness' of mothers to raise their sons, rather than on the sexually violent men. In the final analysis, mothers are blamed, at least indirectly for their son's violence against women (Scully 1990 p66).

Also if a female dominated head were so problematical then as Scully points out we would expect high levels of violence in traditional female dominated societies (1990 p66).

Another criticism that can be placed against placing the blame for crime on the mother based household is that most young men will still have contact with their father. A study I carried out with Ruth Fine into the female membership of the National Council for One

Parent Families found that two thirds of their children's fathers were in contact (Fine and Francome in press). In addition there will be other men even in female headed single person households. There will be brothers, cousins, uncles and grandfathers- all of whom can provide a role model for the young man.

C) **Attitude to the role of the police.**

The right wing tends to be every supportive of the police. We saw in the introduction that Mrs Thatcher said that the Government should back the police and make sure there were enough of them. Furthermore when she came into office in 1979 she gave the force a large pay rise.

If there is evidence of police misdeeds the right will tend to put this down to 'a few bad apples' rather than as evidence of the general corruption of the police. They also value the role of the police. As a left wing analyst told me *'One of the main jobs of the police is to defend property so it is not surprising that the people with property see them as allies.'*

During the 1980s a number of observers have been critical of the fact that the police were used in a more political role and for example, in the miners strike were very much linked with the right wing of the dispute.

D) **The role of punishment.**

The view of the right wing is that punishment is important in order to teach people the error of their ways, to protect the society and to be an example to others who might be tempted to stray. Those who break the law are deviants who need to be punished. In both the two major parties the activists within it are more 'extreme' than the politicians. Consequently those who attend the Conservative Party Conference will tend to be more right wing than the general population, Conservative MPs or Government ministers. A Home

Secretary can therefore gain support by calling for tough action on crime and over the years there has been something of a ritual. Ian Taylor reported: *At the Conservative Party Conference in October 1979, Mr Whitelaw informed a delighted audience that the Government was to introduce new experimental regimes at two existing detention centres for young offenders. Life would be lived 'at a brisk tempo', and young offenders would learn that criminal behaviour would not be tolerated* (198x p25).

Such calls for increased punishment have periodically continued since this time. However, the Conservative Party activists have been disappointed that successive Home Secretary's have not supported the death penalty. To the right wing capital punishment is important as the ultimate threat which will prevent people from re-offending and will make them consider their actions. It will also save the country money.

The New York example In June 1996 the Observer carried a major article detailing the reductions in crime in New York. It argued that the number of murders were down by 40 per cent since 1993 and that burglary had dropped by a quarter. There were 30 per cent fewer robberies and almost 40 per cent fewer shootings. The report continued to say how it was done:

'New York's pugnacious Republican mayor, Rudolph Giuliani, and his police have a simple and empowering answer: they enforced the laws of the land -all of them. Mayor Giuliani's first Police commissioner William Bratton, took office promising a crackdown on so called quality of life crimes such as drunkenness, graffiti and panhandling. The former Boston police chief subscribed to the so-called 'broken windows' theory of policing. His unofficial motto was zero tolerance. The broken windows theory of policing was based on the idea that crime was self perpetuating: leave one window broken in a building and the rest will soon be smashed. Soon the broken windows will create a sense of lawlessness which

will embolden others to commit more serious crime '(Katz and Cohen 1996).

These kind of ideas are similar to those put forward by such right wing academics as James Q Wilson (1983). However, there are some doubts about the effectiveness of this approach. It might lead to police harassment and alienation of the community. Furthermore there were other developments in New York that may also have helped to reduce crime. There was an increased ethos of managerial responsibility and commanders were asked to report what they were doing. There was detailed crime analysis and minor offenders were not only reprehended but also quizzed as to the best ways to deal with major crime (Katz and Cohen 1996).

E) Attitudes to crimes without victims

The right wing tends to regard the social order as vulnerable and so Crimes without victims need to be controlled in order to protect society. For example, in 1994 the Right wing Ian Paisley saw the reduction of the homosexual age of consent to sixteen as a threat:

'The cement that holds society together is the family. As goes the family, so will go the nation. If we don't have the cement of the family, society will disintegrate and be destroyed' (White p6).

In my book **Abortion Freedom** I considered the main different perspectives on the issue and carried out some research into the manner in which beliefs tend to correlate together (1984 p10). Politicians and those who are active in the areas of ideas either for religious or political reasons tend to have clusters of beliefs. Thus a member of the 'Tribune Group' of Labour MPs or the Monday Club' of Conservative MPs would have a particular view of the world and consequent political values. So just by knowing a person is a member of such a group it is possible to predict beliefs and actions over a wide area of topics. In one of my earliest pieces of research in this area I published an analysis of voting patterns of

British MPs on the three issues of capital punishment, abortion and the legalisation of homosexuality (Francome 1978). What it showed was that there were strong correlations. The Third Reading of the Murder (abolition of the Death penalty) Bill was on 13 July 1965 and it occurred two years to the day before the Third reading of the Abortion Bill took place (13 July 1967). One hundred and fifteen Members of Parliament voted both times. Of the eighty one MPs who voted for the abolition of the death penalty four out of five (79%) also voted for the extension of abortion rights and one out of five (21%) opposed them. In contrast of the thirty four MPS who voted against capital punishment only five (15%) voted for the increase in rights of abortion. The activists for the pro-choice groups in discussions would often comment along the lines that *'Those MPs who oppose abortion on the grounds that it is killing nevertheless support capital punishment.'* On the other hand the abortion opponents would sometimes argue along the lines that *'I don't understand why the supporters of abortion agree with the killing of innocent babies yet oppose the execution of those who are guilty of murder.'*

Similar findings occurred in the area of homosexuality. A total of seventy six MPs voted in both the ballots for homosexuality and abortion. Sixty one of these MPs voted to legalise abortion and all but one of these (98%) also voted for the extension of homosexual rights. In contrast of the fifteen who voted against the increased legality of abortion only two in five (40%) were in favour of an extension of homosexual rights.

So the relationship between the three sets of voting patterns is quite clear. However, it is less than perfect and there was more opposition to abortion rights. I carried out further analysis as to the reasons for this and found that a number of MPs who took the generally liberal position on social issues were often opposed to the extension of legal abortion for religious reasons. So of seventeen MPs who supported the abolition of the death penalty yet never the less opposed abortion rights fully ten were Catholics. In an article published in 1978 I attempted to explain why in Britain abortion was still an important political issue and there were votes to restrict it which succeeded in a minor reduction in the time limit. In contrast the homosexuality law was extended and despite the support of the then Prime Minister Margaret Thatcher the repeal of capital punishment was never seriously threatened as it only had the support of the right wing of the Conservative Party. The reason for the added threat to abortion was that in addition to the opposition of those generally conservative there was also the Catholic minority who were generally liberal but on this one issue voted with their usual opponents.

A question arises as to whether similar correlations occurred amongst politicians in other countries. In the United States the situation is different in that the national abortion law was decided by the Supreme Court rather than by the legislature. However, similar groupings of attitudes exist. Those opposed to capital punishment have been more in favour of abortion rights and vice versa. In fact some analysts have broadened the debate to other issues. Although abortion itself could not be made illegal without a change in the constitution there has been a great deal of debate over state financing abortions for poor women. Henry Hyde was the leading opponent of this practice. One of the arguments used by those opposed to the federal finance of abortion and so supporting the Hyde Amendment was their claimed willingness to provide pregnancy support and other family related needs. However, supporters of state finance for abortion noted:

An examination of House members' support for typical welfare policies, like food stamps, child nutrition, and legal services for the poor, raises doubts about this claim. Of those supporting Hyde on abortion, a clear majority, 114 out of 209, consistently voted for cutbacks in welfare programmes. Meanwhile 112 of the 163 members seeking a lenient abortion policy took a lenient line on welfare matters too (Francome 1984 p190).

The report also noted the problem for the supporters of abortion rights in that fifty seven members of Congress who were normally liberal nevertheless voted for the Hyde amendment. Of these nearly four out of five (78%) were Catholics and this finding was similar to that in Britain. In addition to the right wing, abortion had the further opposition of liberal Catholics (Francome 1984 p190).

Although political beliefs correlate together in all societies the nature of the correlation has wide variations. The United States is much to the right of the Europe. This has meant that even politicians in the Democratic Party such as Bill Clinton have supported capital punishment. Whereas, someone with his package of beliefs would not be expected to do so in European countries.

In considering the correlation between groupings of beliefs amongst those who are politically aware, the question arises as to how far such relationships occur amongst the general public. In 1978 I carried out a study amongst nearly a thousand students in New York and I found there was no relationship in the manner that occurred amongst politicians. In fact opinion polls have consistently showed Conservative voters are consistently more in favour of abortion rights than Labour voters while the reverse is true for the politicians. The reason is that the right wing politicians are concerned with threats to the social order while the middle class voters are in favour of free choice and individual rights.

F) The solution to crime

The basic argument is that when there were traditional roles with the man being the honest worker and the woman the home maker there were fewer problems. There was less crime and that which occurred was largely due to poverty and should have disappeared as the social conditions improved. However, the breakdown in morals with the 'permissive sixties' and the changed roles of women, whereby they did not look after children but went out to work instead, had led to a failure in child care. This is complicated by an increase in divorce and a growth in births outside marriage. This means that men are being less responsible in terms of child care and that boys are not brought up with positive male role models.

So to the right wing theorists what is needed is a move back to nineteenth century style attitudes towards sexual attitudes and a restoration of the traditional family. In their view if this were to be then the problems with crime will reduce.

A view of the right wing from the left is provided by Jock Young in an article 'Working class criminology.' In it he argues that those supporting a traditional right wing position generally take the view that the vast majority of people are law abiding. Yet there is a small minority who are 'unambiguously deviant'. To these people deviance is not problematic. The burglar or the marihuana smoker are clearly in the wrong and deserved to be punished. Young drew on Freudian analysis to suggest that they believe 'deviancy is seen as the formless force of the id bursting through a hernia in the superego' (1975 p64).

Right wing academics James Q Wilson and Richard Herrstein argue that there is no such thing as a 'criminal personality'. However, people who commit predatory crimes tend to rank high on two characteristics. Compared to those who do not commit crime or only occasionally offend they are more impulsive- they cannot or will not defer gratification and they are less socialised and display little regard for the feelings of others. Wilson and Herrstein continued to suggest that the family can magnify or moderate any such dispositions. They suggested that a parent can influence the child's development by the process of interaction which involves three processes. First is the development of attachment, the desire of a child to win the adults approval. Secondly, the development of a time horizon by which the child learns to take account of the longer term consequences of its actions. Thirdly the development of conscience and with this an internal constraint against certain actions (1985 p217). So here they were discussing socialisation as a way of reducing crime.

Discussion on the right wing perspective.

There are several weaknesses with the approach of the right wing with its great stress on individual responsibility and punishment. One criticism is that their interpretation is based on a not too closely 'hidden agenda'. Some desire a return to an emphasis on chastity, the nuclear family, segregated roles and examine the facts in the light of this. However, as discussed the fact that there an increase in illegitimacy and divorce was correlated to an increase in crime does not mean the two were causally related. It could well be that an increase in inequality led to <u>both</u> strains on family life and an increase in crime.

A second criticism is that because of their mind set and the fact that they have not really understood what the criminological theories were saying in the 1970s and 1980s they have not considered alternatives. The fact that many parents are not married or living with each other does not necessarily mean that fathers were not playing a role with their children. Many couples not living together still bring up children jointly. Furthermore in the traditional family the man often left such things as visits to the child's school to the mother. However, after separation and the necessary evaluation of their position many men take their responsibilities more seriously. So the solution may not be a return to the traditional nuclear family with traditional roles. On the contrary it may be in the other direction with greater equality in child care and men becoming much more involved whether they are married, single or living together.

Some have suggested that one of the problems with single female households in developed societies contrasted to traditional ones is that there may not be male role models so easily available. In her sample Scully found that among rapists 51% had been abandoned by their fathers by the age of eighteen. When asked who they were closest to in the family 41 per cent of rapists said the mother and only 13 per cent said the father (1990 p67). A more active role of fathers even outside the confines of the traditional two parent family might have benefits to society. In fact one problem with the approach of the right wing to the family and crime is that they ignore the possibility that there could be non conventional families in which the father still plays his full part. In this respect it is interesting to note that Japan and Sweden are two countries which have performed very well in terms of crime indicators. However, Japan has a very low illegitimacy rates while Sweden has a very high one. So the way forward for Britain to reduce crime might be to move more to a Swedish type situation where single women obtain good support and are not in so much poverty and where men play an active role with their children even when they are not married. At the moment there is a great sex inequality in this area and its reduction could lead to much improved crime levels.

The right wing stress the role of punishment in curing crime. They would for example have the society restore capital punishment for murder. However, we can see this approach is very weak in a number of areas and especially in developing an approach to 'terrorism'. We know that normal punishment does not frighten many of those committed to their cause. Capital punishment is not a threat to such men as Bobbie Sands who was willing to starve himself to death for his beliefs.

The 'tough on crime' approach leads to more young men and women going to prison. However, as mentioned in chapter three there is a danger they will learn from those who are more experienced in crime and also become labelled and be less able to take up employment. So a balance needs to be drawn between the protection of society and the problems that will arise by putting high numbers of people in prison.

Many on the right do not consider the social causes of crime. When we characterise the general positions of the right these usually apply to politicians and politically activists. Right wing academics do not always share the attitudes of the political right in, for example, attitude to capital punishment. So we might have more sympathy with the right wing academics such a James Q Wilson who are showing an understanding of the social factors leading to criminality. However, overall the traditional extreme right wing positions has a number of theoretical difficulties and cannot be seen as a solution to crime.

Chapter 5

Marxist approach to crime

This is an area where a number of criminologists have totally misunderstood what Marx, and especially the younger Marx was saying. For example Katherine Williams, in her otherwise very useful text '**Criminology**' states of the espousal of Marxism by the New Criminologists:

'This ignores the oppression which in the twentieth century has been committed in the name of communism; as these regimes began to be dismantled from the late 1980s, such oppressions are seen to have been a clear part of their government. (p381)'

This identification of Marx with reactionary regimes is unfortunate in that the adoption of some of his ideas by these Governments led to many believe that Marx was about repression when in fact the opposite was the case. Marxism is basically about freedom. So in order to understand the Marxist approach to crime we need to consider his ideas and we will use the same headings as for the other theoretical groups.

A) Attitude to major social institutions.

Marx believed that way back in history people lived in a form of primitive communism where the land was owned jointly and where people were co-operating with one another. However, from this early period society was divided into superior and inferior groupings which were always potentially in conflict. Marx mentions the divisions in ancient Rome and those of the middle ages into feudal Lords, vassals, guild masters, journeymen and apprentices (Marx and Engels 1848 p102). These gradations prevented people from freely developing.

He continued to suggest that modern capitalist society sprang from the ruins of feudal society and that within this society new conditions of oppression and forms of struggle had come in place of old ones. Marx's attitude to capitalism was that it was in many ways the worst form of society in that people were exploited by it. However, it also had tremendous possibilities for material development and would lead to the creation of a new form of living.

In this respect one of the crucial factors for Marx was the division of labour. Marx recognised that it led to a great increase in production. He realised that it was very efficient to divide processes up and also noted, that in time, machines would take over the role performed by people. In Capital he provided the following example:

In the manufacture of envelopes, for example, one man folded the paper with the folder, another laid on the gum, a third turned over the flap on which the emblem is impressed, a fourth embossed the emblem and so on; and on each occasion the envelope has to change hands. One single envelope machine now performs all these operations at once, and makes more than 3,000 envelopes in an hour (Marx 1976 ed p540). However, he also argued that the division of labour had negative effects in terms of personality development. He believed that people had tremendous potential and creative talent which was being stifled by society. They were therefore dehumanised by the social system. Given that the right wing in Britain claims Adam Smith to its own and the Adam Smith Institute produces much far right literature, it is interesting to see that Marx quoted him on this very point:

'*The man whose whole life is spent in performing a few simple operations.....generally becomes as stupid and ignorant as it is possible for a human creature to become* (Marx 1976 ed).

It is important to remember the poor conditions under which people lived during this period and the lack of control they had over their lives. In **Capital**, Marx quoted from an official English report which said that the extend of over work done by young people was 'truly fearful' (Marx 1976 p369):

'At a rolling mill where the proper hours of work were from 6 am to 5.30 pm a boy worked about four nights every week till 8.30 pm at least.....and this for six months. Another, at nine years old, sometimes makes three 12 hour shifts running, and, when 10, has made two days and two nights running....Another now 12 has worked in an iron foundry at Staverley from 6am to 12 pm for a fortnight on end; could not do it any more (Marx 1976 p369).

Marx also provided examples of adults being forced to work too many hours. One was of a young woman of only twenty years who died after working 26 1/2 hours in a poorly ventilated room. In addition he pointed out that poets often painted the blacksmith as a hearty person who rose early and slept like no other. However, he commented that they were currently working too hard and in Maryleborne had a death rate of 31 per thousand which was 11 above the mean of male adults in the country. They lost on average a quarter of their natural span and died at 37 rather than 50 (Marx 1976 p367).

So according to Marx the economic and political system was interfering with human and development. This might have been within the overall framework of the legal system. However, to Marx it was clear that the system was unsatisfactory and needed to change.

An important part of Marx's work concerns the role of ideas. Individual people may well think they make up their views based upon a rational consideration of all the facts. However, Marx believed that the role of ideas was limited within the confines of the social structure. One of his favourite phrases was '*It is not the consciousness of men (people) that determines their existence, but, on the contrary, their social existence determines their consciousness'* (Marx 1848 p11,12). He believed that people's ideas would in large measure depend upon their position within the social structure. However, the dominant ideas would belong to those with the greatest power. In <u>The German Ideology</u>, he said:

'The ideas of the ruling class are in every epoch the ruling ideas, i.e. the class which is the ruling material force of society, is at the same time its ruling intellectual force. The class which has the means of material production at its disposal has control at the same time over the means of mental production (Marx 1974 ed p64).

So Marx was right to identify the fact that in all societies the elite with its control over the mass media would spread certain ideas which would help to legitimise its position and reduce political dissent. One such belief is that those with ability can get to the elite positions of society and so the system is basically fair. In the United States we see this view encapsulated in the view that the average citizen can go from '<u>log cabin to the White House</u>'.

Marx's view of religion is related to his other theories. One part of it regards religion as a reflection of people's alienation. Those people who were alienated could not become their true selves and so therefore needed to idealise a God figure. Once alienated existence was ended so would the need for religion. Marx commented:

'The abolition of religion as the illusory of men (people), is a demand for their real happiness. The call to abandon their illusions about their condition is a call to abandon a condition which requires illusion.'

The second part of his theory of religion was related to his theory about the role of ideas. So, if the upper class could persuade the working class not to worry too much about life on earth because they were bound to have such a good life in heaven, then the workers would be much more willing to accept their condition rather than to work for social change. However, if the workers believed they had only one life to lead they would be more likely to fight for improved conditions. Marx also believed that religion was a great comfort to people in their alienated condition.

'Religion is the sigh of the oppressed creature, the sentiment of a heartless world, and the soul of soulless conditions. It is the opiate of the people (Zeitlin ND p96).

So Marx was critical of society and given the social conditions of the time he was right to be so. He believed that the working class would eventually all receive the same level of income and united would take power from the elite. The country would then be run in the interests of the vast majority. By this time capitalism would have developed so much wealth that material shortages would not be much of an issue and labour would as far as possible be humanised.

B) Attitude to the family.

In the Communist Manifesto 1848 Marx and Engels argued for the abolition of the family as it was currently constituted:

'Abolition of the family! even the most radical flare up at this infamous proposal of the communists.

On what foundation is the present family, the bourgeois family based? On capital, on private gain. In its completely developed form this family exists only among the bourgeoisie. But this state of things finds its complement in the practical absence of the family among the proletarians, and in public prostitution.

The bourgeois family will vanish as a matter of course when its complement vanishes, and both will vanish with the vanishing of capital. Do you charge us with wanting to stop the exploitation of children by their parents. To this crime we plead guilty. But you will say, we destroy the most hallowed of relations, when we replace home education with social.

The bourgeois claptrap about the family and education, about the hallowed correlation of parent and child, becomes all the more disgusting, the more, by the action of modern industry, all family ties among the proletarians are torn asunder, and their children transformed into simple articles of commerce and instruments of labour.... Bourgeois marriage is in reality a system of wives in common and thus, at the most, what the Communists might possibly be reproached with is that they desire to introduce in substitution for a hypocritically concealed, an openly legalised community of women'.

In considering this evidence Fletcher states that it reveals that Marx and Engels were not totally against the family. Rather the they were opposed to the kinds of family amongst the richer segments of the society (1988 p55). At the time Marx and Engels wrote, women had on marriage to hand over any property to their husbands. So Fletcher stated that Marx and Engels were in particular attacking the subordinate status of women and also the fact that well off men resorted to prostitution.

Another point made by Marx and Engels and considered by Fletcher was that the working class family did not exist as the exploitation of the proletariat was so extreme that the family could not thrive within it. One of the main purposes of their attack was to improve the status of women and stop them from being 'mere instruments of production' (Fletcher 1988 p56). So Fletcher argued this work does not actually call for the abolition of the family as such but rather the abolition of the bourgeois family and the social conditions that prevented the development of the proletarian family.

He also said evidence that Marx did not oppose the family came from his personal life.

'One had to have sees Marx with his children in order to get a full idea of the depth of feeling and childishness of this hero of science. In his minutes of leisure or on walks, he carried them about, played the maddest merriest games with them- in brief was a child among children. On Hampstead Heath we often played 'cavalry'. I took one of his little daughters on my shoulders, Marx the other, and then we vied with one another in trotting and humping-on occasion there was also a little fight between the mounted riders' (Fletcher 1988 p77).

This evidence shows Marx in his father role but does not undermine Marx's criticisms of the family as it was constituted.

C) The causes of crime.

Marx took the view that sometimes the changes in the capitalist system were such that jobs would be destroyed or changed to such a degree that people would not be able to adapt. They would then not be able to work for a living but would have to engage in deviant behaviour. In Capital he talked of some employers evading the factory acts leading to idleness *'which drove the youths to the pot-house, the girls to the brothel (1867 p291)'*. Capitalism would produce conditions which would cause crime and prove to be a threat to the social order.

Marx and Engels knew that a number of criminals were popular amongst the masses. There was support for those such as Robin Hood who was believed to steal from the rich to give to the poor. However, Marx took the view that generally crime had negative effects. He suggested that capitalism threw up a subsection of the working class called the lumpenproletariat. This he regarded as a parasitic group which was living off the productive labour of others by committing crime or arranging activities such as prostitution.

The interests of this group are diametrically opposed to those of the productive workers. They may also be open to being bribed to work for the state against the interests of the workers (Hirst 1975 p216). Modern day left wing criminologists take a similar point of view and Lee and Young pointed out that criminals were much more likely to steal from their own class than from the elite (1993).

We have seen in chapter one that some on the left have argued that capitalism is bound to lead to crime which must therefore be considered as a normal reaction to a propertied society.

Another aspect of Marx's view of crime was that the ruling class would use the State to define as criminals some of its political enemies within the working class. They would try and ignore the political nature of the actions and stigmatize their actions as crimes (Hirst 1975 p220).

Quinney developed this aspect of Marxist analysis to more modern conditions. He argued that in capitalist societies such as the United States the ruling class, although being divided on some matters, nevertheless has interests apart from those of the rest of the society. One of its primary aims is to preserve the capitalist order both at home and abroad. In other countries the power of the United States army helps to attack any foe which may try to upset the foreign markets. At home the criminal law is used to prevent any challenges to the capitalist order and is in the hands of ruling class (Quinney 1975 p195). This is not direct, however but is through the role of the state. *'Crime control becomes a major device of the State in its promotion of a capitalist society'(1975 p196).*

D) **Attitude to the role of the police.**

The attitude of Marx and later Marxists to the police is generally negative. They take the view that the police are members of the working class who have betrayed their own interests and gone over to serve the interests of the upper class (Francome 1976 p280). One example of this kind of police activity is provided by Hirst. After the 1848 attempts at revolution the Prussian government tried to destroy the communists by pretending they were engaged in a conspiracy to overthrow the established order. They fabricated minutes and documents and Marx worked to expose the fraud. His wife, Jenny commented:

'All the allegation of the police are lies. They steal forge, break open desks, swear false oaths...claiming they are privileged to do so against Communists, who are beyond the pale of society' (J Marx 1852 p72, Hirst 1975 p221).

A number of Marxists stressing this aspect of the role of the police have been very opposed to them. Jock young's study of students found that 93% of Marxists contrasted to only 34% of other students agreed with the statement that 'The police by their very nature are liable to act in a vicious and brutal way' (1968 p166-71). However, some Marxists take a view that the negative identification of the role of the police is too simplistic and that it has a wider role. Paul Q Hirst for example comments:

'The police force in our own society is not merely an instrument of oppression, or of the maintenance of the capitalist economic system, but also a condition of a civilised society under the present political economic arrangements' (1975 P240).

He continued to state that any Marxists who did not recognise this would be siding with thieves and murderers.

E) **The role of punishment.**

To Marxist academics such as Quinney the role of punishment is as a method of social control by the upper classes through the state. However, from Marx's work it is clear that he differentiates between political actions designated as crimes and common theft which is counter revolutionary.

F) **Attitudes to crimes without victims.** The quote from Marx about religion being the 'opiate of the people' shows much about Marx's view of drugs. Drugs may be used by those in power to anaesthetize
the population and so stifle dissent. They should therefore be opposed.

Marx believed that such things as drug taking and prostitution were often sponsored by the 'lumpenproletariat'. Instead of working they live off the 'crumbs of capitalist relations of exchange' (Hirst 1975 p216). Hirst argues that while Marx regarded 'theft' very negatively because the thief produces nothing the prostitute may in some circumstances be regarded as a productive labourer.

'The prostitute who sells for his/her personal support is an unproductive labourer, like the tutor or the lawyer who works on his own behalf. The prostitute who provides the same services for a wage in order to make money for an entrepreneur is a productive labourer, like the singer whose performances enrich a theatre owner' (1975 P227).

Marx saw prostitution as an activity which preceded capitalism but as the quote shows could in certain circumstances produce surplus value.

Marxists in recent years have tended to favour the rights of the individual in terms of birth control and abortion. However, in the nineteenth century the way the population debate was presented led to Marx and the dominant socialists being opposed even to birth control. As I have documented more fully in my book **Abortion Freedom** the early controversy over birth control dated back to the French Revolution. Godwin in his *Enquiry Concerning Political Justice* argued that the causes of injustice were the human institutions which needed to be changed by the removal of the inequalities in society. Malthus attacked this view, contending that if Godwin's type of utopia came into existence there would be such a massive population increase that the standard of living would take a precipitous fall. This argument appealed to the upper classes who were terrified that the French Revolution would be repeated in Britain and were looking for a justification of the existing order. Marx in his *Capital* rightly talked of the Malthus theory as being *'greeted with jubilation by the English Oligarchy'(1976ed vol 1 p766)* and he also called it a *'shameless plagiarism (1976ed p639).'* From this and other information it became clear that in the nineteenth century birth control was identified with the reactionary forces. The solution to poverty was not to redistribute wealth towards the poor as the socialists wanted but rather to persuade the poor to have only as many children as they could afford. During the First World War the birth control activists agreed that they would begin to spread birth control information on the basis of free choice and socialists became more active in support.

It was a country claiming to be Marxist-the Soviet Union- which first legalised abortion. The most eminent society of physicians had called for all laws to be removed in 1914 and in 1920 the country did so. Many medical visitors reported on the relative safety of the operation which influenced practice in the rest of the world. The growth of Stalinism led to the repeal of the Soviet Law in 1936. The New York Times reported this was against the wishes of the women who felt they were to be 'childbearing machines'(Francome 1984 p63).

So overall the attitude of Marxist's to 'crimes without victims' depends on their relevance to the struggle for social change.

G) **Marxist approach to curing crime.**

To Marx the whole system of capitalism was a crime. Its dehumanising parts would lead to people being oppressed and not able to attain full personality development. In the communist manifesto he said that people were born free but everywhere were in chains. The fact that people stole under capitalism could be acceptable, for example Marx, like most people, would understand if a poor mother stole to feed her children. However, Marx also saw other crime that would be due to poor personality development due the capitalist system. In this case it might be excused although regrettable

There is a passage of Marx's work in which he recognised that criminality may give rise to art such as Shakespeare's Richard the Third. He continued:

'The criminal breaks the monotony and everyday security of bourgeois life. In this way he keeps it from stagnation' (Hirst 1975 p222).

He also impishly noted how crime could lead to inventiveness

'Would locks ever have reached their present degree of excellence had there been no thieves? Would the making of bank-notes have reached its present perfection had their been no forgers. Would the microscope have found its way into the sphere of ordinary commerce but for trading frauds' (Hirst 1975 p222).

In this kind of passage Marx seemed to be taking a position not far from that adopted later by Durkheim where we have seen crime was seen as 'normal' and had functions for society. However, the difference is that Marx foresaw a time when property crime would disappear. Marx believed that capitalism would develop to such a degree that it would remove material wants and it would then be possible to humanise labour so there was little alienation. People would be able to develop their personalities freely. In the Communist Manifesto he said that in place of the old society with its class antagonisms there would be an association in which *'the free development of each is the condition for the free development for all'*.

In a famous passage he explains that a crucial change would be the abolition of the division of labour. In the Communist Manifesto he talked of people moving out to live in the countryside so that the distinction between town and country was diminished. The social changes would be such that in the new society people would not have an exclusive area of activity but could become accomplished in any branch they wished. In **The German Ideology** Marx said the new society would bring freedom and make *'it possible for me to do one thing today and another tomorrow, to hunt in the morning, fish in the afternoon, rear cattle in the evening, criticise after dinner, just as I have a mind, without ever becoming hunter, fisherman, herdsman or critic* (1844 p64).

People would come to realise that the accumulation of goods was not the main aim of life so there would be no need to spend such a great amount of life in production. Rather the central aim of life should be the development of personality and personal relationships. Each person would contribute to life what they had to give and would receive their material needs from the society. Hence Marx looked towards the day when society could inscribe on its banner: *'from each according to their ability to each according to their need'* (1848).

Marxists maintain that in such a society there would be little reason to engage in crime. There would be sufficient wealth that people would not need to steal and the quality of life would be so well developed that there would be few social strains. In 1916 the Marxist, Bonger maintained that under capitalism people were encouraged to compete with each other and to be self seeking. This could easily lead to crime. However, in a different kind of society people would live together in harmony. In 1973 **The New Criminology** was published which argued that over nineteen out of twenty offenses were property crimes. Consequently if a new kind of society were developed where there would not be the concern with wealth then virtually all crime would be eliminated. Taylor, Walton and Young concluded their book with a discussion of the fact that society and social relations could be transformed leading to the eradication of crime.

Discussion

There is a great deal of value in the Marxist perspective. It is very useful in helping to understand the underlying forces in society. In the nineteenth century especially, many people believed that their views were based on a rational view of events. What Marx showed was the social nature of opinions. Marx and Engels also attacked the poor social conditions present at the time and revealed the extent of poverty.

The weakness of the Marxist theory is that it has never been tested. There has never been a truly Marxist society, although many claim to have been one. We have therefore been unable to test his theory. However, the point made about varying social conditions leading to different rates of crime is clearly correct. We know now that even within a capitalist societies there are great variations in levels of crime. If we can identify the social conditions leading to low levels of crime it will provide us with guidelines for action.

Marx's theory of how a revolution can occur has not been born out empirically. As discussed Marx believed that the working class would become a large homogeneous group and that after the revolution the great mass would rule in the interests of the vast majority. This theory needs to be revamped in the light of subsequent experience because history has shown that times of social stress in a pre-revolutionary situation throws up many groups. The situation in Iran was classic in that a variety of groups joined together to produce change but after the revolution the groups who fought together fought each other.

One of Marx's quotes was that people should contribute towards society what they can. We can agree that if people were geared to contribute what they could towards society rather than to see what they could get out of it then crime would diminish. We can see echoes of this in Jack Kennedy's Presidential speech when he told young Americans to: 'Ask not what your country can do for you-but what you can do for your country'. If we can create a society where there is more altruism there is likely to be much less crime. This line of argument will be continued in the final chapter.

Chapter 6

The Centre ground and crime

We have seen that the extreme left and right take a totally different perspective on crime. The central ground which is occupied by the right wing of the Labour party, the Liberal Democrats and the left wing of the Conservative Party show many similarities. For example they all oppose capital punishment and this is one of the reasons that this is not an important political issue in Britain. They all take a liberal position on crimes without victims such as abortion and homosexuality but not on drugs. The politicians more to the centre well may attack their 'extremists'. So left wing Conservatives may well the disagree with extreme right. For example, we have seen that right wing Tories have tended to label one parent families as a cause of crime and there were moves to cut their benefits in 1993. The former Prime Minister Ted Heath attacked this *'the Government will only be penalising children who are already likely to be substantially disadvantaged.*(1993 p24)'

On some issues politicians of the centre have come together to fight the 'extremes'. In fact there have been two notable issues where right wing conservatives and left wing Labour politicians joined together. The first of these was the reform of the House of Lords when Michael Foot and Enoch Powell fought successfully together against reform and the second was the membership of the Common Market where both extremes were opposed to membership. We can envisage other more crime related issues where this could occur in the future. For example both the left and right wings might oppose more prison building. For the left wing it might be because they did not want to send more people to prison and for the right wing they might want conditions in prison to be more uncomfortable to act as a deterrent.

As discussed in Chapter four, in general the activists in the Labour Party and the Conservative Party are more 'extreme' than their party leadership. So the move of the Labour Party towards 'New Labour with its dropping of its commitment to wholesale nationalisation will mean that many of its activists will be disappointed. Left wing politicians have been put in the position where they have had to accept some policies which they do not like in order to obtain some change on the theory that 'half a cake is better than none'.

This also applies to the Conservative Party. Its delegates at the Party conference will be much more right wing than the general population. Consequently the policies that the party will probably want in its manifesto to increase its vote are likely to be to the left of the policies supported by the activists. Although Britain since 1979 has been in an unusual situation because the economic policies have been largely to the right despite the fact that the majority of people voted against the policies. This was in large part been due to the nature of the British electoral system and the splitting of the 'moderate' vote between the Labour and the Liberal Democrats.

Some similar considerations apply to the United States. In 1996 the delegates to the Republican Convention were more to the right than the rest of the country as indicated by their attitudes to abortion. Although there are some left wing anti abortionists we have seen that it is mainly an issue supported by the right. A Washington Post survey found that 72% of the Republican delegates believed that abortion should be 'illegal in all or most circumstances'. This was much higher than the figure of 52 per cent for registered Republicans and 41 per cent for all registered voters. To appease the Christian Right the Republicans were putting forward a policy of total abolition of abortion and the fact that it does not have widespread political support helps explain why the issue was kept from being a main one at the conference (Walker 1996a).

The wily ex-republican President Richard realised the importance of this kind of analysis on the differences in views. As the

<u>Observer</u> reported:

'The disgraced former president told Dole that he would win the party's nomination by pandering to the right. To win the White House, however, he would have to turn sharp left and head for the centre. That said the grizzled old master, is where presidential candidates find the golden ten per cent of swing votes that decide American elections' (Freedland 1996).

The report also stated that one reason that Bush lost in 1992 was that publicity was given to arch right winger Pat Buchanan's call of a culture war against, gays, feminists and half the American people'. Of course another factor was the fact that the right wing vote was split by the third party.

Capital punishment is the one issue that does not fit in with a left/ right analysis. The general population has always been in favour of it. This was so much the case that Sheila Hogben, of British Gallup told me that during the period up to the abolition of the death penalty in 1966, the organisation refused to conduct polls on the issue. It felt these would give ammunition to the opponents of reform.

Since abolition in Britain there has not been any real threat of the death penalty returning. The Home Secretary, in office in 1996 - Michael Howard- said that he had voted in favour of Capital punishment until 1990. He changed his mind because of evidence of miscarriages of justice such as that of the Birmingham six. He stated *'We cannot but be relieved that the death penalty was not available when we consider the plight of those who have been wrongly convicted '*(Bates 1996).

In the United States capital punishment has returned and the failure to endorse it was seen by many as a crucial factor in the defeat of Dukakis in the 1988 Presidential race. President Clinton faced no such handicap, although if he were in Britain his attitude to capital punishment would not sit easily with his general political position.

Realist Criminology Academically a number of left wing thinkers moved more to the political centre. In her book 'Criminology' Williams comments;

'The most important writers in this field are British, people like Jock Young, Roger Matthews, Pat Carlen and John Lea. Two books are invaluable to the discussion of this subject, each is a collection of essays published in 1992: Rethinking Criminology: the realist Debate edited by Jock Young and Roger Matthews; and Issues in Realist Criminology edited by Roger Matthews and Jock Young' (1994 p408).

The approach of realist criminology is to consider all aspects of crime rather than concentrating on one or two aspects as earlier theorists had done. We have seen that the positivists and the right wing concentrated on the individual, the Marxist approach concentrated on the role of the state and we shall discuss also the role of labelling. Left realism identifies four major groups of factors as particularly important. These are: offenders, victims, formal controls such as the police and other agencies of the state and informal control by which is meant the public. These four facets can be identified as points on a square (Williams 1994 p409).

For the realist criminologist full consideration of crime entails

* Analysis of why people commit crimes

* The role of the state in delineating what are the crimes.

* Why and in what ways the state controls behaviour. The role of the police and prisons. The unintended consequences of actions.

* The interaction of different social groups in society.

* The reasons for changes in policies.

They maintain a combination of all these factors help provide a rounded explanation of crime. This movement of criminological theory towards the centre ground is likely to make it more politically relevant. It is beginning to recognise the complexity of society and the fact that any explanation of the causes and treatment of crime will depend on a combination of factors. We have spent a great amount of time on the right and the far left. Let us now consider the political position of the left/centre ground.

The Labour Party and Crime The Labour party has put forward a number of proposals on crime which we can consider as an example of the middle position albeit left of centre. Tony Blair Commented in the Sunday Telegraph:

'Human beings have free will, the choice to act well or badly. What distinguishes me from Conservatives is that I believe people are more likely to act well and improve themselves in a society where opportunities are offered to them to do so; which strives to be cohesive and treats people as of equal worth. This, I think is the crucial difference between my own position and the Marxist and Tory extremes' (1996a p1).

In another article the position of Labour was summed up by Tony Blair as being 'tough on crime and tough on the causes of crime' (Blair 1996). Those holding this position recognise individual responsibility for crime but also consider problems such as poverty, relative and absolute deprivation. They argue that, despite the fact that we can understand that some people have received poor socialisation, they must still generally be held responsible for their actions. Let us further consider their position using the same categories as for the far right and left.

A) Attitude to major social institutions.

The social order is unfair is that there is a great amount of inequality which can lead to poverty. The state has a role in eliminating the worst excesses. Tony Blair has been stressing 'one nation' politics and the idea of a *'stakeholder economy which involves all our people, not a privileged few, or even 30 or 40 or 50%'(Blair 1996 p3)*. He continued to say that the development of an underclass living in poverty, with high levels of crime and family instability is a moral and economic evil. Rather he looked towards a unified society with a strong sense of purpose and with all the people working together as a team (Blair 1996 p4). So the attitude towards the major social institutions is that they must be improved in order to better serve the needs of the community.

B) Attitude to the family.

In a Fabian pamphlet David Utting argued that when the government drew attention to the relationship between families upbringing and delinquency they were in tune with popular sentiment. He argued that opinion polls show that the public generally thinks that parents rather than the government were to blame for the increase in juvenile crime. He continued to say that there had been a recent tendency to link rising crime with the seven-fold increase in the divorce rate in the past thirty years and the fact that now nineteen per cent of families are headed by a lone parent. However, he argued that some of the figures that had caused anxiety were in a fact a misrepresentation. For example the Sunday Times had announced that two parent families with dependent children accounted for only one in four households and that 'the abnormal family has now become the norm'. Utting argued that this apparently shocking fact becomes less so if it is realised that over six out of ten homes are occupied by childless couples and single people. So unless single people are abnormal such claims are absurd. In fact Utting continued to say that seven out of ten families in this country are headed by both natural parents, one in five are one parent families and around one in twelve are step families. Families headed by a single mother account for only one family in sixteen.

He drew attention to a Family Studies Centre Report which followed children up in longitudinal studies. These found that a number of family factors were significantly linked to later delinquency. The study also showed that those children who offended at the earliest ages were the most likely to be recidivists and to be more likely to engage in violent crime. The related family factors were identified as follows:

1 Poor parental supervision

2 Harsh, neglectful or erratic discipline.

3 Parental discord.

4 Having a parent with a criminal record.

5 Low family income.

6 Social disadvantage including membership of a large family.

7 Aggressive and troublesome behaviour at school.

He was at pains to point out that these factors were not predictors but did help to identify those children that might be at risk. He gave as an example a study of Newcastle families and the fact that 70% of those assessed before the age of five as 'deprived and receiving poor domestic care' were eventually convicted of a criminal offence. He, however, counselled that if young children in a poor environment were stigmatised it would be problematical. This would be not only because some of the children would not turn to crime, but also because others equally at risk would be missed.

Similar evidence is provided by an article in the BMJ. Shepherd and Farrington argue that in some ways the society socialises its young into crime:

'*At age 8 the best predictors of subsequent offending are hyperactivity, impulsivity, and attention deficit; marital discord between the child's parents, harsh or erratic parenting; and socioeconomic deprivation. Separation from a parent for reasons other than death or illness is also important. Evidence from studies on vulnerability and resilience shows the importance of the cumulative effect of risk factors in the development of delinquency*' (Shepherd and Farrington 1995 p271).

The evidence seems to show that risk factors for subsequent offending and being apprehended are cumulative. Shepherd and Farrington maintain that children with two risk factors are four times as likely to become offenders as those with one or none.

<u>One parent families and crime</u> Utting argued strongly that '*the obsession with family structure-by which I mean whether children are living with one parent or two*' was not a way of approaching crime prevention (1994 p7). There is not the evidence to link one parent families with delinquency and he provided the following information:

* An analysis of 50 British and American studies suggested that children who had experienced divorce were perhaps 10 -15 per cent more likely to engage in delinquent behaviour than children from intact two parent homes. Even then the kind of acts were heavily weighted towards such crimes as under age drinking or truancy rather than serious crimes.

* A Home Office (1985) study of teenagers and their mothers failed to find a statistically significant difference in behaviour between either boys or girls from one parent families compared to those from intact two parent ones.

* Joan McCord followed the behaviour of US men first observed as children in the 1940s. Those who were from intact homes where the parents were in conflict were nearly twice as likely to offend compared to men brought up by a single affectionate mother. The author's conclusion to the study was:

'The quality of home life rather than the number of parents affects crime rates' (Utting 1994 p7).

* A Cambridgeshire study of the delinquent development of 400 boys born in South London in 1953 found that the experience of divorce before the age of ten was associated with juvenile offending. However, it was the authors view that it was the conflict between the parents which was the significant background factor.

So Utting suggests that discord between parents is one factor leading to stressful situations in which children are not given the support they need.

C) **Attitude to the role of the police.**

In contrast to the Marxists the centre ground believes the police have an important role to play in maintaining order in society. The Labour Party is a pains to be seen to give support to the force, although many of its left wing will be critical of aspects of police behaviour. Lea and Young point out that for the police force to be successful it needs a measure of public support. They draw attention to a study of policing in Britain where nine out of ten (89%) of crimes were reported by the public and only six per cent were directly detected by the police (1993 p62). One problem they identify with the police is racism which can lead to unnecessary harassment of young blacks and lead to alienation and crime. However, they are to the left of the Labour Party. The Party itself is likely to see examples of racism as being due to a few prejudiced members of the police force.

A Fabian Special entitled <u>Facts for Socialists</u> stated that around 1990 the police forces were overstretched partly as a results of the poll tax which took up the time of 1,700 officers to police (Wright 1991). It continued to say that a Labour government would increase the number of police officers on the beat and would make them accountable to their local community (1991 p23). So the police were regarded as potential allies.

D) **The role of punishment**.

The Labour Party in saying it is going to be 'tough on crime' aims to distance itself from the position of the radical left which often sees prison in a negative light. In Chapter Four the approach to crime in New York was discussed and the Shadow Home secretary Jack Straw has lent this approach some support. He called for a crackdown against *'winos and addicts whose aggressive begging affronts and sometimes threatens decent compassionate citizens'* (Katz and Cohen 1996). This stress on the individual as a cause of crime is a move away from the structural explanations of the left. It may also be seen as having the potential to work in certain circumstances as there have been some practical examples of this approach. Birmingham council imposed a ban on drinking alcohol in public places in 1988 and this was seen as helping to 'tidy up' the city centre. Although there was some evidence of displacement in that some of the hardened drinkers were seen to harass people in provincial parks. Overall, furthermore, there are some doubts about the effectiveness of this approach. It might be successful in some circumstances but lead to police harassment and alienation of the community in others.

The one issue where the centre ground in British and US politics differs greatly is on Capital punishment. When a vote to restore it was taken on 21 February 1996 none of the Labour Party was in support, nor were the left wing Tories or Liberals. It was only the right wing of the Conservative Party and the Irish MPs who were in favour. In contrast in the US all Republicans solidly support the death penalty and even the right wing of the Democratic Party does so too.

E) **Attitudes to 'crimes without victims'**

It was during the Labour tenure of office during the 1960s that abortion was liberalised as was consenting homosexual behaviour between men over the age of twenty one. These were both private members bills but did have the tacit support of the government and were given extra time. In 1994 Tony Blair, the current leader of the Labour Party, made a strong speech in the House in favour of reducing the age of homosexual consent to sixteen. It failed by 27 votes. The majority of Conservatives voted against the measure and the majority of Labour members supported it.

The failure to reduce the age of consent from twenty-one to sixteen led to a vote to reduce the age to eighteen which passed. This proposition was supported by virtually all the Labour MPs but four out of ten Conservative MPs opposed the change. Of 154 opposing any reduction in age limits 134 were Conservatives. Most of the Conservative cabinet including the Prime Minister voted against an age limit of sixteen but in favour of one at eighteen (McKie 1994). So we can see that on this issue as in other areas of 'crimes without victims' Labour MPs are more supportive.

F) **What is the crime solution?**

The view of the Labour Party is that the social order is unfair is that there is a great amount of inequality which can lead to poverty. The state has a role in eliminating the worst excesses. Professor Peter Townsend has argued that the ratio of disposable income in this country between the richest 20 per cent and the poorest 20 per cent is ten times. In contrast it is only four times in Japan. This, he argued, is in large part because Japanese management has accepted more realistic salary awards. He continued:

107

'Is it too much to ask for £10 billion a year to be shifted back from the top ranks to the bottom ranks during the first five years of Labour's next term of office? That could be done without penal rates of personal taxation-by means of new emphasis on social services, gaps in necessary benefits filled, tax expenditures sharply reduced, subsidies for private insurance removed, corporation taxes fixed at average European levels, the top contribution rate of earnings towards national insurance and SERPS raised, and steps taken to moderate excessively high earnings' (1996 p6).

So from this view of the dominant Labour thinkers it is crucial to move towards a more equal society and when this is achieved the crime rates will be reduced.

The Labour Party has had other ideas for reducing crime. These include caretaker schemes on estates, improved street lighting and more staff on public transport (Wright 1991 p23).

Discussion

The realist criminologists are taking a much improved approach to that of many criminological theorists in the past and at last there are some signs that the centre ground is considering a variety of methods to help reduce crime. It is wisely putting forward an approach to crime which considers both the role of socialisation and that of punishment and rehabilitation.

A little thought will show that children born in the United States today will have little difference in hereditary from those born in Britain. However, they will be far more likely to commit violent crime which suggests that a much higher proportion in the US are socialised into violence. This could point for the need of more help being given to families whether they be of the one parent or two parent variety.

Chapter 7

Labelling and Crimes without victims

Becker (1951) noted that certain subcultures have totally different norms from the rest of the society. The dance band musicians he studied had their own value system which in some ways was antipathetic to the dominant belief system. Their social life was very different from that of the average person. They did not have regular hours of work and leisure, and their family life was fragmented. They were often smokers of marijuana and had different attitudes towards music. The kind of songs they played as part of their work were relatively straight 'middle of the road', while when they jammed together they played much more complicated music.

In some respects they were regarded as deviants and Becker took an extremely relativistic view towards this. He commented:

Social groups create deviance by making the rules whose infraction constitutes deviance, and by applying those rules to particular people and labelling them as outsiders. From this point of view, deviance is not a quality of the act the person commits, but rather a consequence of the application by others of rules and sanctions to an 'offender' (1963 p9).

So Becker regarded the process of interaction as important between the person who commits an act and those who respond to it. However, in his view there is no objectively deviant act. What is deviant at one time and in one place will not be deviant in another place or in the same place at another time. So a second question is who makes the rules and here Backer suggests the important thing is political and economic power. The more powerful make the rules for the less powerful to follow. So the young are made to follow the rules of the old, women follow the rules of men, blacks must follow the rules of whites, the working class must follow the rules of the middle class and so on'(1963 p17).

Another important feature of the rule makers in Becker's view is that they are moral entrepreneurs. Becker writes that the crusader:

'Operates with an absolute ethic; what she/he sees is truly and totally evil with no qualification. Any means is justified to do away with it. The crusader is fervent and righteous and often self righteous. It is appropriate to think of reformers as crusaders because they typically believe their mission is a holy one (1963 p148).

In his analysis of the moral entrepreneur, Becker leaned heavily on Gusfield's analysis of the American Temperance Movement and took the view that the moral crusader can often have strong humanitarian overtones. Gusfield divided activists into two groups. The assimilative reformer was sympathetic to the plight of the urban poor and hoped to persuade the drinkers to raise himself to middle class respectability and lifestyle. In contrast the coercive reformer is not interested in socialising the deviant into new ways of thinking but rather to use the law to enforce the values of the dominant group. Gusfield pointed out that those who wanted to keep their values dominant were able to ensure that certain crimes were proscribed.

Criticisms of labelling theory

The new criminologists criticised Becker's work. They pointed out that, while it is true that the act of killing someone could be regarded as patriotism or murder according to the social context, there are limits within which these labels are acceptable. They said that patriotism is a social definition largely limited to war time (Taylor, Walton and Young 1973 p146).

Alvin Gouldner was a consistent and fierce critic of Becker in large part because he argued the approach avoided conflicting with the existing sources of power (Gouldner 1971 p379). In his view Becker's work only attacked low level officials within a welfare system and avoided conflict with high levels officials who shaped the character of the institutions.

I believe that Becker's work is instructive and clearly some young people do become labelled and subject to deviancy amplification. However, it is most relevant for the area of 'Crimes without victims' and it is to this issue that we now turn.

Crimes without victims

In his book with this title Schur argued that there were a group of offenses in which there were no complainant. These include drug use, prostitution, homosexuality in some countries, consensual under age sex and abortion. Schur argued for the decriminalisation of these kinds of issues because the law should not be used in these areas;

The more cogent issue is not whether we approve or disapprove of the behaviour in question, but rather whether we approve or disapprove of efforts to curb them through the criminal law (Schur 1974 p10).

He suggested that there were many adverse affects of laws against victimless crimes. The fact that there is no complainant means that they are unenforceable. They create large profits for the providers of the services and provide poor quality merchandise. They can, furthermore, lead to a disrespect for the law both because people will be breaking it on a regular basis and because the underground culture can lead to police corruption. He also stressed the class availability of the services. Schur set out to answer some of the criticisms that could be raised by opponents:

'Many persons would contend that these situations do involve victimisation. The drug addict, they would argue, is a victim of his condition; the prostitute is victimised by her condition; some would assert even that the fetus is a victim in the case of abortion' (1974 p4).

Against these kinds of arguments Schur stated that the persons involved do not regard themselves as victims. In fact he argued that in large part the efforts to control human behaviour by means of criminal legislation have been due to a wish to achieve ends and maximise values believed essential for social well being (1974 p4).

Historically, we have seen it has been the left who have been the most supportive of 'crimes without victims'. However, there is by no means any necessity for this to be the case. I carried out a series of studies of public opinion of abortion with Gallup and other organisations during the 1980s and consistently found that Conservative voters were more in favour of the right to choose an abortion than the average. It was the Conservative politicians who were more likely to be opposed to it. In my earlier work I suggested that this difference was probably due to the fact that the politicians were concerned with social order what the voters were concerned with individual choice (Francome 1984).

There have been signs in the 1990s that many right wing politicians both in Britain and the USA have moved towards giving freedom of choice in the area. In fact there is a case for 'crimes without victims' being decriminalised from a Conservative perspective. Schur realised this and include in 'Victimless Crimes' a quote from the book endearingly entitled *'The Honest Politicians Guide to Crime Control'*.

'We must strip of the moralistic exescrences of our criminal justice system so that it can concentrate on the essentials. The prime function of the criminal law is to protect our persons and our property; these purposes are now engulfed in a mass of other

distracting, inefficiently performed legislative duties' (Morris and Hawkins 1972).

So there is nothing necessarily radical about Schur's perspective in terms of challenging the wider order of society. Let us consider three areas of importance as crimes without victims:

a) Abortion The question arises as to whether abortion is really a victimless crime. It is clearly so from Schur's definition for there is no complainant. However, there is an argument that the fetus is a victim and some people will argue that a fetus deserves all the legal protection afforded to a child. Indeed at one time it used to be argued by the Catholic Church that a pregnant woman should die rather than have a termination. So a book published with Church approval and in its fifth edition in 1935 stated quite clearly:

'To preserve one's life is, generally speaking , a duty, but it may be the plainest duty, the highest duty, to sacrifice one's life. War is full of such instances, in which it is not man's duty to live, but to die.....a parallel case, is the situation of a woman in a difficult labour, when her life and that of her unborn child are in extreme dangers. In this situation it is the mother's duty to die rather than consent to the killing of her child.' The author, the Rev Patrick Finney, continued:

The first fact in the world is that justice, law and order, should be observed no matter what the cost, better that ten thousand mothers should die than that one fetus be unjustly killed (Finney 1935 p46).

The British Medical Journal reported one doctor who had eight women die over a twenty five year period because they had refused or been refused interference with the pregnancy (11th December 1937).

These days childbirth in the developed world is now generally much more safe and so this not so much of an issue. However, there are important issues surrounding abortion. I wrote a book **Abortion Freedom** which documented the fact that many countries were legalising abortion (Francome 1984). However, it is a crime in many societies and is proscribed by many religions. In countries like the United States there are continued debates both over whether it should be made illegal and over issues such as state funding for poor women and the rights of minors (under 18s).

For further discussion of this issue students are referred to my books of which there are multiple copies in the library (1984, 1986)

B) Homosexuality

Homosexual male prostitutes were a feature of life in Victorian England. Chesney Comments:

'It seems that active male homosexuality was less socially obtrusive in the middle fifty years of the nineteenth century than either before or after. This may have been that social forces produced fewer practising homosexuals. Apart from those who are unambiguously inverted, there are always many men whose desires can be directed either to women or to other men, and the intense pressures of mid-Victorian England would certainly have pushed them towards 'normality' (1970 p327-8).

One of the facts that may have made homosexuality less noticeable was the fact that the fear of heterosexual activity was so great that people did not worry about men bathing naked together or entering each other's bedrooms.

Things changed somewhat with the 1885 Amendment Act which made buggery a serious criminal offence and introduced what some people called the 'blackmailer's charter'. Since that change in the law we have seen several distinct approaches to homosexuality.

a) The first is to regard it as a criminal offence. In Britain this lasted until 1966 and is still the case if homosexuality occurs in Northern Ireland, in the armed services or amongst consenting men under the age of eighteen.

b) A second approach is to regard it as a sickness. The idea is that homosexuals have not developed properly and need to be cured.

c) A third stage is to regard it as an alternative lifestyle. This is the position taken by those like Ken Plummer in his book **Sexual Stigma** and developed in his later works.

This looked like becoming the widely accepted position before the spread of AIDS led to homosexuals being blamed. This I have discussed more fully elsewhere (Francome and Marks 1996 pp165-178).

c) Under age sex and teenage pregnancy

The Government's target is to reduce to rate of teenage conceptions from a national average of 9.5 per thousand girls aged 13-15 to no more than 4.8 by the year 2,000. The Chief Medical Officer's annual report for 1990 estimate that almost half of all conceptions were unwanted or unintended (Department of Health 1991 p94). The use of conceptions instead of births was an important development because the majority of those conceiving under the age of sixteen would be over that age by the time they gave birth.

The changes in conception rates for all teenagers and those aged under sixteen can be tabulated as follows: Refer Table 7.1

Table 7.1 shows that the conception rate for the under-sixteens the increase was 40% over the same period until again there was a fall in 1991. The figures also show that in 1991 52% of conceptions among the under-sixteens ended in abortion. Amongst all teenagers 34% of conceptions ended in abortion.

It has been noted by previous researchers that there is a link between social inequality and levels of teenage conception. In Glasgow it has been reported that teenage births made up 2-4% of all births in areas characterised by high proportions of professional and managerial residents and 20-25% in areas of high unemployment and social deprivation (Rosenberg and McEwen 1991 p173). A study in the North Thames Regional Health Authority found first that there was a wide discrepancy in pregnancy rates according to social status. In 1990 Tower Hamlets, an area of high social deprivation, had a conception rate amongst 16-19 year olds of 95 per thousand. This contrasted to 37 per thousand in Hampstead. It also found that teenagers in deprived areas were much less likely to obtain an abortion. So a pregnant teenager in Tower Hamlets was four times as likely to continue the pregnancy as a similar teenager in Hampstead. This study concluded by saying that a cycle of deprivation is being perpetuated and that teenage mothers and their offspring were becoming a substantial part of an urban underclass (Garlick, Ineichan and Hudson 1993).

Out of 178 health districts in England only 5 out of 178 met the Government's target 4.8 per 1,000 under sixteen conceptions in 1991. These were Tunbridge Wells 3.6 per 1,000 women aged 13-15, Northallerton 4.2, South West Surrey 4.3, Harrow 4.3 and Wycombe 4.4. All these areas are places with little poverty. In contrast at the other end of the scale two districts had rates four times the Health of the Nation target. These were North Manchester with a rate of 19.9 and Hull 19.2. Other districts had rates exceeding 15, which is more than three times the targets. These were Grimsby 16.9, West Lambeth 16.7, South Manchester 16.5, Hartlepool 16.0, Doncaster 15.7, Central Manchester 15.4, Camberwell 15.4, Salford 15.3, and Sandwell 15.3. In Wales none of the nine districts met the targets. The lowest rate was in Powys (6.1) which had a rate which was under half the conception rate of Mid Glamorgan (13.1) (OPCS 1994 p18). We do not have comparable data for Scotland. Overall many districts with these excessively high rates must be considering what action to take to meet the targets.

Our survey of young teenage mothers

In August 1993 I was requested by the Family Planning Association to carry out some research into teenage pregnancy for a report and presentation on the TV show **World in Action.** The programme duly appeared on 4 October 1993 under the title 'Children who have Children' and a preliminary report was published by the FPA at the same time. The sample was made up of young women aged seventeen and under who had recently had babies or who were pregnant and continuing the pregnancy. The questionnaires were administered by the heads of special units providing education for pregnant mothers and schoolgirls. In all we asked 130 young women to fill in the questionnaire and 129 did so. This gives a response rate of over 99% and is indicative of the women's wish to co-operate with the study. We asked the young women about the quality of their sex education. Refer Table 7.2

The results show that the best information was provided on periods with nearly two in five having good information. However, 13.6% had no information. Just under three in ten (28.2%) reported having good information about condoms. The lowest approval rating from the young women was on the matter of relationships and only one in nine said that they had received good information on these.

Experience of first sexual intercourse

We asked about the reasons for starting sex. The question wording was as follows: '*Could you please think back to when you first had intercourse and tell us the reason why?'-Circle as many of the following that apply to you.*' Refer Table 7.3

The teenagers gave an average of 1.9 reasons each. By far the highest one mentioned was 'in love'. This was the reason stated by three in five overall and more than two thirds of the younger group. The second most often mentioned reason was 'got carried away' with nearly three in ten identifying this factor. Almost as many mentioned 'curiosity' which appears to be a crucial supplementary reason.

In the younger group 12.6% said that they were drunk and 5.6% said they were raped. Overall, however, very few said that they were under pressure from their partner.

We were interested in the age at which sexual intercourse began for our sample and so we asked *'How old were you when you first had intercourse, and how old was your partner?'* Refer Table 7.4

The results show that the partners of the young girls were much older. If we consider the youngest group who were aged fifteen and under we see that two thirds (67.2%) of their partners were over sixteen and almost one in five (17.9%) were over twenty. If we consider the older group aged sixteen and seventeen only 7% waited until sixteen for their first experience of intercourse. Yet 57% of their partners were over the age of sixteen.

Birth control use at first intercourse

We asked the sample: *When you first had sex did you or your partner use any form of contraception? If so what?* The results can be tabulated as follows: Refer Table 7.5

The results show that the teenagers used largely 'male' methods of birth control, over a half said that they use either the condom or withdrawal. Over two in five of the sample did not use a method of birth control at all but about one in ten of these wanted to get pregnant or were ambivalent about it. So a sixteen year old living with her partner and her four-and-a-half-month-old baby said *'I knew if I got pregnant it wouldn't bother me, as I knew he would stay with me'*. Less than 6% used female methods of birth control. Typical comments on non-use were *'It just happened'*. *'I thought it would be alright'*. Some mentioned non availability of condoms: *'It just happened and we didn't have anything on us '*.

Partners in Pregnancy

A second question on age of partners asked about the partner's age at the time of pregnancy. Of 129 girls in the sample 126 responded to this question. One of the three non-respondents said she did not know the age of the father. Refer Table 7.6

The results show that 120 (93%) of the women had under age sex. They also showed that in 113 (90%) of cases the man was older. In ten cases they were the same age (in completed years) and in three cases only, the boy was younger. The average age of pregnancy for the girl was 14.5 years while the average age of their partners was 18.2 years.

The results show that for the 117 girls who became pregnant before the age of sixteen, over four out of five (81%) of their partners were over the age of sixteen. Indeed over a quarter (26%) were over the age of twenty and two were aged twenty-seven. Given the fact that condoms were most often mentioned as the method of birth control, this finding suggests that great inroads could be made into young teenage pregnancy if young men aged 15-30 could be convinced of the necessity to wait until the young women were aged sixteen or to take precautions, the most practical method being the wearing of a condom. A much greater use of condoms among young couples has the potential to provide significant reductions in unwanted pregnancies, sexually transmitted diseases and would help to limit the transmission of HIV.

Discussion Labelling theory (or interactionism) does help in explaining societies reaction to some areas of crime. However, it

119

is much too relativistic to have to much value outside of the area of crimes without victims. This preliminary discussion has briefly introduced three of these. Prostitution will be considered in chapter twelve and drugtaking has also been discussed at various points in the text.

There are those who would follow Schur in suggesting that Crimes without victims should be decriminalised. However, there is a strong question of political feasibility. There is, for example, a case for legalising many of the recreational drugs so that their use could be monitored, taxes could be raised and the quality could be assured. Furthermore possible negative effects on health could be more easily researched. However, such a change would not have public support and would open the politicians involved to criticisms of undermining public order. In other areas there are important ethical issues. There is a great difference in aborting a fetus at six weeks gestation from one at six months which would probably be viable outside the womb. Consequently the law will need to take a position under what conditions abortion should be legal. The laws on under age sex, whether heterosexual or homosexual will cover a wide variety of situations. There is clearly a great deal of difference in two fifteen year olds having sex as part of a development of their romantic relationship and the exploitation of a fourteen year old child by a much older person. Society has always had rules to protect its young and vulnerable members and on some occasions a balance must be drawn between such considerations and providing freedom of the individual.

Chapter 8

Rape and society

This chapter will first of all consider some factual, legal and theoretical aspects of rape before considering the reasons for its rise in recent years and making some proposals as to how it might be reduced. In a controversial passage Barbara Toner commented:

There is a fantasy, cherished by women as well as men, that men must struggle frantically to overcome their natural instinct to rape and that women, after resisting, respond with a passion they didn't know they had. It rests on the assumption that rape is the result of an overpowering sexual need, a male need, experienced only by women who are nymphomaniacs. Yet there is no proven physiological reason to explain man's greater sex drive. Although his greater aggression might possibly be biologically accounted for, anthropological evidence suggests that the strength of the sex drive, male or female, depends largely on the demands of individual cultures (Toner 1982 p50).

Barbara Toner continued to say, however, that rape was in reality not really a sexual act. Rather it is a hostile act of aggression. Scully, adds to this explanation of rape two others which have been put forward in the past. These are that it is a disease and a neo-Freudian one that rape is precipitated by the victim. These are considered below. However, first we shall consider some epidemiological factors.

Prevalence of rape Scully suggests that between 25 per cent to 50 per cent of rapes are unreported. In one study of 246 victims of rape in Seatle who contacted a rape crisis centre 100 had not reported their rapes to the police. Scully also suggests that women are more likely to report the rape if it is of the classic kind where a total stranger invades a woman's home or attacks her in a public place (1991 p6). She therefore comments:

121

Rapists in prison, then, are more likely to have raped strangers, used weapons, physically injured their victims, and committed other crimes in addition to the rape(Scully 1990 p7).

This figure by Scully is likely to be conservative. In 'Sane New World' I commented:

One point to bear in mind is that the official figures are a gross underestimate of the number of rapes. Researchers estimate that only about one in five are reported and I would be inclined to put the figure lower than this. I have known six women who were raped and one of these was working in a drugs project in Brooklyn and was raped in a short period of time. The second occasion happened in broad daylight and she did not tell anyone- not even the man she married- for over five years. I would suggest a reportage rate of about one in eight in Britain and a lower figure in the United States, maybe one in twelve (Francome 1990 p100).

There are two reasons for expecting a lower reportage rate in the US. First many of the rapes occur amongst women in minority groups who are alienated from the police. Secondly the clear up rate for rape in the US is only just over half compared to four out of five in Britain. Going to court is a very harrowing experience for the rape victim and very often the evidence is not believed (Francome 1990 p100). A British doctor gained wide publicity in November 1988 when he claimed that one in three allegations of rape is false. Dr Gillian Mezey of the Maudsley hospital commented that the remark had undermined the attempts of psychiatrists and volunteers working with women to convince them that it was worthwhile reporting attacks and that their claims would be believed. She drew attention to a New York study which found the rate of false allegations to be only two per cent which is comparable to unfounded complaints in other criminal offenses (Francome 1990 p101).

There is no doubt that rape and other violent attacks against women are a great problem. A study in the Islington area of London by Jayne Mooney published in 1987 found that in terms of non sexual assault, women were 40% more likely to report attacks compared to men and that one woman in five knew of a female who had been attacked in the previous twelve months. This was despite the fact that women took many more precautions than men. They were, for example, five times more likely to never go out after dark, three times as likely to avoid certain people or streets and six times more likely to always go out accompanied rather than alone (Francome 1990 p101).

In Britain young white females are twenty-nine times as likely to be assaulted than those over the age of 45 and 30 times as likely to be sexually attacked.

In the United States the national data show that two in five women do not feel it is safe to go walking most places at night. Johnson calculated the lifetime risk of rape to women aged 12 and over. He conservatively estimated that 20 to 30 per cent of young girls aged twelve years will suffer a violent sexual attack during the remainder of their lives. He said that such a common occurrence cannot be based on the behaviour of small minority and commented:

'Instead the numbers reiterate a reality that American women have lived with for years: sexual violence against women is part of the everyday fabric of American life (Johnson 1980 p146).'

The data for 1986 showed that in the USA women aged 16-19 were more than thirty times as likely to be raped as those over the age of 35 and that black women were twice as likely to be raped as white women. In part this latter figure may be the results of poverty as women with incomes under $7000 are fifteen times as likely to be raped as those with incomes over $50,000 a year (Francome 1990 p102).

The USA data for the late 1980s also showed wide variations in rates of rape over the country. The highest rate was in the State of Alaska with 73 per 100,000 population, followed by Nevada and Michigan. The lowest rate was in Iowa with a rate of 12 per 100,000. So a woman in Alaska had six times the possibility of being raped as one in Iowa (Francome 1990 p117-8).

Medicalisation of rape

In addition to the 'uncontrollable impulse' cause of rape we have seen that Scully proposes there are two others which we shall now consider. There was for many years a great influence of the medical model. This led in 1965 to thirty states and the District of Columbia having laws defining the rapist as *'a person unable to control his sexual impulse or having to commit sex crimes'*(Scully 1990 p35). In the US psychiatrists experimented with a number of techniques to try and control rape including castration, electric shock therapy, mind control drug therapy as well as psychotherapy (Scully 1990 p36).

This kind of medicalisation of rape tends to regard it as an explosive impulse which the men involved are at a loss to control. In Freudian terms it would be the id overcoming the ego and super ego. This image of rape fits in with some of the popular beliefs about male behaviour. As long ago as 1951 Karpman argued:

Sexual psychopaths are, of course, a social menace, but they are not conscious agents deliberately and viciously perpetrating these acts, rather they are victims of a disease from which many suffer more than their victims (Karpman 1951 p190).

However, such empirical evidence that is available does not support this position.

A good piece of research was carried out by Amir. He followed the Gluecks (1956 p94) in dividing rapes in Philadelphia into three categories. These were 'planned', 'partially planned' and 'explosive' (Amir 1971 p141). in planned rape the criminal either enticed the victim into a position where the act could be perpetrated or alternatively a plan was made to coerce her into sexual relations in a place where she was known to be going to be. In partially planned cases, plans were hastily drawn after the offender encountered the prospective victim and plans were quickly drawn up. In an explosive situation there was no forethought but the perpetrator decided on the act on impulse possibly with alcohol impairing the criminal's judgement (1971 pp141-2). Amir suggested that in reality it was sometimes difficult to distinguish between the three categories. However, he found that a out of 646 rapes 72 per cent were planned, 12 per cent were partially planned and in 16 per cent of cases it was an explosive event. His results according to place of occurrence can be tabulated as follows: Refer Table 8.1

The results show that over two thirds of the rapes were planned and that this was true for wherever people first met. The highest case of explosive rape occurred in the victim's home, however, even then it was less than a third. Where the victim met the offender in the open, less than ten per cent of the rapes were categorised as explosive.

Blame the victim

Amir states that some observers have argued that a woman can resist rape because of the position of her sexual organs (1971 p161). However, he argues that there are a number of situations in which rape could be possible:

a The disproportion in physical size between the woman and her attacker

b the victim could be in an unconscious state or intoxicated.

c the element of surprise which dissipates resistance.

d A threat which prevents further resistance.

e fear of bodily harm from blows.

The final reason he gave, however, was of a different order and it was:

'the unconscious desire of the victim to, or apathy to intercourse with a stranger. Moreover, although people tend to view rape as an act which befalls the victim without any cooperation, or reciprocal action on her part... in sexual offenses the victim may not be free from all complicity in the act and sometimes the so called victim is a consenting party' (Amir 1971 pp161-2).

Scully suggests that psychoanalytic theory could be used to discredit victims. That within this theory the 'core female personality' exhibits three characteristics. These are narcissism, masochism and passivity. On the question of masochism she quotes Karen Horney:

The specific satisfaction sought and found in female sex life and motherhood are of a masochistic nature. The content of the early sexual wishes and fantasies concerning the father is the desire to be mutilated, that is castrated by him. Menstruation has the hidden connotation of a masochistic experience. What the woman secretly desires in intercourse is rape and violence, or in the mental sphere humiliation (Horney 1973 p24, Sculley 1990 pp42-3).

This approach seems to be most unlikely. There is little if any evidence that women are more masochistic than men. Indeed if all the adverts one sees for 'Miss Kane' and such like in the telephone boxes in central London it may well be men who are most masochistic. This approach has great dangers in that it can be used as a justification for violence against women.

126

Littner following this approach distinguished between 'true victims' who did not wish to be raped and 'professional victims' who had a masochistic desire to be raped despite the fact that they were not aware of it. Their unconscious desires mean they *unwittingly cooperate with the rapist in terms of covertly making themselves available to him (1973 p28, Scully 1990 p 43')*. This approach is also to be regretted and should not have been put forward without clear evidence that it is true. One may ask if people who are mugged have an unconscious desire to have it happen. We may also ask about rapes of males by other males. There were several examples of this in London and by all accounts the victims were left traumatised.

This analysis is of more than academic interest. In a well known case in 1983 a woman went into Big Dan's Bar in New Bedford Massachusetts. She was attacked and raped by a group of men in an incident which lasted over two hours. Other men prevented the bartender from calling the police. The initial sympathy was with the victim but when she went to buy the cigarettes she had left her children at home and people began to blame the victim. A total of 16,000 people signed a petition asking for leniency for the rapists. One woman was quoted *'They did nothing to her. Her rights are to be home with her two kids and to be a good mother. A Portuguese woman should be at home with her kids and that's it'* (Chancer 1987 p251, Scully 1990 p53).

Role of the police

'During the war I use to walk my husband to the station at three O'clock in the morning so that he could get the last train to be back to the navy the next day. We were never sure that this was the last time we would be together and so we waited until the last minute. I then use to walk home. I never thought about being attacked or raped it never entered my mind'.

This comment in 1994 from a seventy year old woman shows a change in attitudes and perspectives. These days any woman walking around alone would be open to criticism for being foolhardy. Indeed we shall see that the police would be very critical of her behaviour.

The advice given by the police to women can lead to them being blamed. The document **Positive Steps** produced by the Metropolitan Police around 1992 gave advice to women as to how to avoid attacks. It said to try to avoid walking home alone. However, if it were inevitable the advice was;

* *Don't take short cuts.*
* *If the street is deserted walk in the middle of the pavement.*
* *Always walk facing on coming traffic to avoid curb crawlers.*
* *If you think you are being followed cross the road and keep walking. If he continues to follow you, make for a busy area or well lit house to ask for help.*
* *Don't wait around unnecessarily, but if you have to, look confident and positive.*
* *Keep you hands out of your pockets so you are always free to defend yourself.*
* *Plan your journey so that you avoid using deserted bus stops. Never be tempted to hitch a lift.*

For women drivers the advice included:

* *Stay in the car as much as possible. Keep the windows closed and the doors locked.*
* *If you think you are being followed, try to alert other drivers by flashing your lights or sounding your horn. Or keep driving until you come to a busy place, a police, fire or ambulance station or pub.*
* *At night, park in a well lit place. Lock up, putting any valuables in the boot. And when you get back, remember to check the back seat before getting in. Have a good pocket torch handy*

and the keys ready in your hand for a quick getaway. consider carrying a personal alarm with you.

In the United States, the national data shows that two in five women do not feel it is safe to go walking in most places at night. The advice from the police is to be careful about their movements. The proposals from the police in Nassua County, on Long Island just outside New York were more forthright than that from the Met:

Don't hitchhike, avoid deserted areas. Don't walk close to buildings, alleyways or shrubs, walk aggressively, walk near curbs and in lighted areas, avoid shortcuts, carry keys between your fingers ready to use them, travel with a companion and if you feel you are being followed run for it (Francome 1990 p101).

Women in cars were as in London advised to always check the back seat before entering, not to pick up hitchhikers, if they were followed they should lean on the horn and drive to a populated area. They should keep doors and windows locked while parking or driving, if a tyre bursts they should ride on it. Other advice was:

If the car breaks down lock the doors, display a white cloth and ask whoever stops to call the police. The problem is that this kind of advice implies a siege mentality and has dangers in that any woman who does not carry out all these precautions is likely to be blamed as being foolhardy, even if she is only exercising her right to do things for herself such as mend her own tyre. So this kind of information can lead to the victim taking the blame and also to women being placed in very traditional subordinate roles. So there are a variety of ways that women may be blamed for what is an offence perpetrated by males.

The wife's fault

In some psychoanalytic literature the wives of rapists have been blamed for their husbands actions. Scully points to the work of

129

Abrahamsen who analysed eight women who had suffered abuse from their rapist husbands. He argued that such men often choose wives who unconsciously desire sexual abuse and are fulfilled by it. He also argued that these women were also competitive and aggressive and that the husband who rapes was the victim of the wife. In a passage which does not increase the standing of the psychological profession he argued:

There can be no doubt that the sexual frustration which the wives caused is one of the factors motivating the rape which might be tentatively described as a displaced attempt to force a seductive but rejecting mother into submission. The sex offender was not only exposed to his wife's masculine and competitive inclinations, but also in a certain sense, was somehow seduced into committing the crime (Abrahamsen 1960 p p165, Scully 1990 p44).

This kind of explanation is lacking in perspective and, of course, cannot explain the high numbers of rapes by single men.

The feminist approaches

One strand of feminist theory on rape is that put forward by Susan Brownmiller in her best selling book 'Against our Will'. This book contains a history of rape including many examples of women being raped after their men had been defeated in wars. She commented:

'From prehistoric times to the present, I believe rape has played a critical function. It is nothing more or less than a conscious process of intimidation by which all men keep all women in a state of fear (1975 p5).

Jane Caputi has similarly discussed the role of rape in keeping men in the dominant position in a patriarchical society:

Rape is a social expression of sexual politics, an institutionalised and ritual enactment of male domination, a form of terror which functions to maintain the same quo (1987 p3).

In summarising one strand of thought since her book Hanmer and Maynard concluded in 1987 that feminist research pointed to the fact that inequality, oppression and power were allotted along gender lines and that violence is used to control women. In this sense all men benefit not just those who actually rape.

It is not clear why men benefit if women are raped because it means there are unnecessary restrictions on women in society and men will suffer too by a climate of fear. They will face the fear of women and so have to be extra careful not to frighten them. They also will have extra concern for the well being of their daughters, partners, mothers, friends and indeed all women who may be attacked.

In the United States where the rates of rape are much higher there has been more concern with the issue. In 1986 in the book Abortion Practice I argued that there was a cultural difference and US men were more likely to be assertive and unconcerned about women's feelings. Margaret Mead's work on the societal differences during the second world war proposed that the fact there was evidence that US men were less likely to wear condoms shown that they were taking less responsibility for the possibility of an unwanted pregnancy. Furthermore such phrases as 'barefoot and pregnant' which suggests the role of sex and pregnancy in ensuring that a woman is kept within her traditional role, is one that does not occur in Britain. It is only a phrase, but it is possible that it is illustrative of a difference in attitude between the cultures and a greater hostility towards women in the US.

There is other evidence of the strong sexual divisions in the United States. In 1978 I asked a random sample of 797 single students aged 17-20 two questions on casual sex. One of the questions asked students where they agreed with the following statement: 'Boys should not go to bed with someone they have just met, for example, at a party.' Only one in five of the young men agreed with this compared to three in five of the females. The males were also more in favour of the females having casual sex. Only three in ten of them said that girls should not go to bed with someone they had just met at a party, compared to seven out of ten of the females. So the sexual divide was very marked and easily statistically significant. However, it was not the traditional double standard where males wanted to be sexually active themselves and marry a virgin or at least someone relatively innocent. Both males and females showed a large degree of consistency, but the males were clearly socialised to pursue a much more liberal attitude towards sexuality than the females. (Francome 1986 p177) The work of Roberts points in the same direction:

All the relevant British and American inquiries have found that young people worry about personal relationships, particularly their ability to 'sell' themselves to the opposite sex....It becomes part of the currency in sexual negotiations. Girls sell favours and boys pay out, the terms of trade being set by the partners' relative ratings. Youth cultures mediate wider social mores, and teach females to use their sexuality to build social relationships, while males learn to use sex for personal gratification, and pay with status earned in the wider society (1985 p80).

It appears that although double standards operate in both societies, nevertheless various structural and historical factors make the difference in standards far less marked amongst the British. This was particularly the case with students. For example the British grant system meant that for the three years they are at university both male and female students had a similar amount of money and so the traditional patterns of relationship with the male paying for dates and providing transport could not be maintained. There is also a differences between Britain and the US in terms of youth culture. The British culture is much less competitive than its US counterpart and, while there is a strong double standard, there is not the same need to succeed sexually. As discussed elsewhere:

The fact that peer groups are against members spending too much time with girls means those who have little success with members of the opposite sex can find comfort in being loyal peer group members. It is therefore possible to be a social success without dating on a regular basis or having a regular girlfriend. In fact, the groups are rather censorious of those who are too involved in relationships. This is a crucial difference from the situation in the United States and is linked to the lack of competitiveness in the British culture over a wide range of activities. The peer groups stress equality and are supportive of their members (Francome 1986 p179).

Taking the USA analysis further Doyle argued that there are five elements in the male gender role in the United States. These are:

1 An anti feminine element-the dislike of anything connected with the feminine.

2 The success element-being number one, numero uno.

3 The aggressive element- the willingness to fight.

4 The sexual element- constant and insatiable desire for sex.

5 The self reliant element- being tough, confident, independent and cool

To these Scully adds another:

6 Hostility towards women. This she tested on the grounds of distrust, dislike and threat.

For example, Scully found that three quarters of both her groups

133

of men believe that a man should not give up when a woman says no to sex (Scully 1990 p85).

There is also hostility from women towards men. In 1979 one story that was retold by a group of feminists was of a biologist who worked in a laboratory;

One day she was attacked and raped by four men. She pretended not to get angry but asked them to take her back to her home where she would give them coffee. Once back she slipped drugs into their drinks and while they were asleep castrated them all. This story seems a little unlikely. However, the point is that it was retold and her actions greeted with such phrases as 'right on' (Francome 1986 p184).

One of the concerns of the feminist movement particularly in the US, is the concern about date rape. The issue sprang to importance in 1985 when Ms magazine ran a story on rape in US universities: <u>Date rape: The story of an Epidemic and Those Who Deny It</u>. The story claimed that one in four college women is the victim of actual or attempted rape (Roiphe 1994 p54). More fuel to the fire was added with the William Kennedy Smith date rape trial in 1991.

One of the plans of the feminist movement was the idea of combating date rape by reclaiming the night with marches. These in US universities became very emotional with demonstrations, speeches with recollections of sexual abuse and slogans (Roiphe 1994 p30):

No matter what we wear no matter where we go
'Yes' means 'yes' and 'no' means 'no'!

Roiphe continued to say that the march had a cathartic release as individuals told their stories (p37). Columbia's 1992 speak out lasted from nine at night until nine in the morning (1994 p48).

Divisions in the feminist movement

The 'anti all male' parts of some thinking has been attacked by Elizabeth Wilson in Britain. She criticised the work of Brownmiller by arguing that her statement about 'all men being potential rapists does not account for the widely differing kinds of rapes between societies. More recently criticisms have been made by Katie Roiphe in the USA. In her book Roiphe, an alumni of Harvard and Princeton, argued that feminism, which had started in order to give women a voice, was now being used to tell them what they ought to think and say. There was in her view a confusion towards radical and conservative attitudes towards sex. In this respect she quoted a poem of her mothers.

If a candle burns at both ends
It will not last the night
But ah my foes and oh my friends
It gives a lovely light.

Her mother had introduced her to feminism, however, Roiphe argued that, with the epidemic of AIDS, her mother had become much more conservative and argued that people should not have sex any more unless they were in a long-term serious relationship (Roiphe 1994 p27). She argued that the feminist motives had become mixed up with a fear of sex and aids and a fear of men. She also had doubts about the functions of the demonstrations:

I remember myself, a bewildered freshman, watching candle-lit faces weave snakelike through campus. Angry voices were chanting 'Two, four, six, eight no more date rape,' and the marchers carrying signs saying 'Take Back the Night'. I remember an older student from my high school, whom I'd always respected, always thought particularly glamorous, marching, her face flushed with emotion, and I wondered ..... whom they wanted the night back from and what they wanted it back for (Roiphe 1994 p11).

However, she stated, although women claimed they could not walk out at night, the figures show that men were more likely to be attacked. At Harvard in 1992 out of 29 instances of assault and battery reported to campus police 21 of the victims were male.

Roiphe was also critical of some of the ideas in the US that a man must not simply have unspoken consent. A former director of Columbia universities date rape programme told New York magazine that each time intercourse occurs the man must have explicit consent and that without it rape has occurred. Roiphe comments that such a position is not realistic and is retrograde in its assumptions about how men and women react together. In her view it is also reactionary in at least two ways. First it implies that women are unable to communicate what they want and cannot assert themselves in a relationship. Secondly, it seems to promote a view of sexuality where man is always 'on the make' and yet women have no real sexual desires:

The assumption embedded in the movement against date rape is our grandmother's assumption: men want sex, women don't. In emphasising this struggle-he pushing, she resisting- the rape crisis movement recycles and promotes an old fashioned view of sexuality' (1994 p63).

She was also critical of some of the suggestions that colleges should go back to single sex dormitories which she said would be putting colleges back into the 1950s (1994 p64). She scorned another idea that male professors should only see female students alone if the door to their room is open or that they should have a chaperon. She said these changes would lead to the idea that professors are more interested in their students bodies rather than their minds (Roiphe 1994 p95). In support of her case against the US rape crisis feminist's attempt to create a desexualized women she quoted Germaine Greer. In 'The Female Eunuch' Greer had said that it was often falsely assumed that sexuality was *'the enemy of the female...In fact, the chief instrument in the deflection and*

136

perversion of female energy is the denial of female sexuality for the substitution of femininity or sexlessness (1971 p59, Roiphe 1994 p84).

Anthropological evidence

Peggy Sanday (1979) found rape was present in just over half tribal societies. In the sample 51 out of a total of 95 (54%) tribal groups showed evidence of it. Other observers have found rape more common. For example Broude and Green (1976) found it present in three quarters of societies- 26 out of 34 (76%). Sanday suggested that rape was part of a culture of violence and male dominance. One point the anthropologists made was that in preindustrial societies economic power helps to enable women to obtain immunity from men using force against them. Scully comments:

Anthropological research suggests that sexual violence is related to cultural attitudes, the power relationship between women and men, the social and economic status of women relative to the men of their groups, and the amount of the other forms of violence in the society (Scully 1990 p48).

In her book **The Facts of Rape** Barbara Toner also discusses some anthropological evidence:

The Arapesh

This group, who lived in the Mountains of New Guinea were studied by Margaret Mead in the 1930s. Mead stated that they survived by a spirit of co-operation. Although they had different sex roles, there was nevertheless not the aggression and competitiveness characteristic of some other societies. Both the sexes worked together for the community.

In part because of their taboos, in their attitude towards sex there was a reticence to proceed if the conditions were not correct. Both partners should have been willing and sex occurred as part of a relationship. Mead commented:

Of rape the Arapesh know nothing beyond the fact that it is the unpleasant custom of the Nugum people to the southeast of them. Nor do the Arapesh have any conception of male nature that might make rape understandable to them (Toner 1982 p52, Mead 1932).

The Gussii

This group who were Bantu speaking farmers living in the highlands of Kenya were studied by Robert Levine in the 1950s. There were seven tribes who were generally hostile to each other. However, they needed each other because the tribes were exogamous and so brides had to move from one to the other. The group's attitude to sexuality reflected the social structure and Toner summarises:

The wedding night sexual performance is of immense importance to the status of both husband and wife. The husband is determined to force his wife into a position of subordination by repeated acts of intercourse, preferably to hurt her so much that she is unable to walk the next day. The bride is determined to resist to the utmost, to bring shame of on the husband. The act of intercourse is seen as an act of subjugation of the female and as such it continues to be important in the marital relationship (1982 p52).

This group had very high rates of rape. In 1955-6 they recorded 47.2 rapes per 100,000 population and this was known to be an underestimate. At the time the rate of rape in England and Wales was less than a tenth of this figure.

Toner continued to argue that the high levels of rape were likely to be due to the patterns of relationship within the society and between the sexes. There is a separateness and hostility between men and women stemming from childhood experiences (1982 p53). In her view British culture was much more akin to that of the Gusii than the Arapesh. She stated that women often have different motives for sex than men. The woman may well agree to make love from motives springing from romantic ideals of love and giving. However, her seducer's motives might well have been concentrated on taking. Consequently the woman might end up feeling used and even perhaps abused.

She identitied the fact that the social development of men and women is such that it encourages separation, ignorance and antagonism. Men and women are socialised into different roles.

Men are encouraged to be assertive and sexual success is to men a sign of social success. Toner provided quotes from two authors which in a sense capture some of the differences in a nutshell. DJ West commented in his book 'Understanding sexual attacks' in 1978:

The culture, and more especially the working class culture, defines masculinity not merely in terms of sexual virility and copulatory expertise, but also expects male to display assertiveness and competitiveness as well as physical strength, courage and willingness to stand up and fight (West 1978, Toner 1982 p54).

In her book 'Educating Adolescent girls' published in 1981 Eileen Chandler commented:

Almost everything girls understand about society trains them from the earliest days to be huntresses, to catch their man, and they are taught to do it by being gentle, sweet, loving and pretty. But at school they are taught to be competitive, aggressive and to try to beat boys at their own game. Being intellectually able isn't what attracts men and people don't like girls to be pushing (Toner 1982 p54).

She argued that despite a certain amount of belief in sexual equality the images from the media were still very conservative. Suspense movies are usually about the helpless woman because violence against women is more thrilling.

Morgan Trial

Pressure for change in the law on rape came in 1975 with the trial of Morgan- a thirty-seven year old airman accused of aiding and abetting the rape of his wife. On the evening of 15th August 1973 Morgan spent his time drinking with three younger members of the RAF who were all in their twenties. The men had tried to pick up women in Wolverhampton but had failed and Morgan invited them to his home to have intercourse with his wife. The three younger defendants said that Morgan had said his wife was a little kinky and would struggle a bit but that this turned her on. The woman was asleep in a single bed in a room with her eleven year old son when she was woken up by the four men. The incident was described by Barbara Toner:

They woke her and frog marched her into the next bedroom where there was a double bed. She struggled violently and screamed and shouted for her son to call the police, but one of the men held his hand over her mouth. She was held on the bed by her arms and her legs while each of the younger men had intercourse with her while the other two 'committed various lewd acts on various parts of her body'. They left the room and her husband forced her to have intercourse with him. When it was all over she grabbed her coat, ran out of the house, drove straight to the hospital and made an immediate complaint of rape to the staff. (Toner 1982 p131).

At first the defendants made statements to the police corroborating the story but later in the witness box they said that she consented to the intercourse and positively joined in the activities. The defence was that there was no lack of consent and secondly that if there were, they were not aware of it.

The judge directed the jury that if the defendants believed, or may have believed that Mrs Morgan had consented to the intercourse then they were not guilty of rape. However, the belief had to be held honestly and secondly it had to be reasonable- such as that would be accepted by a reasonable man if he sat down and thought about it. The jury did not accept the defence and the men were sentenced to long periods of imprisonment. They appealed, however, on the grounds that the judge had misdirected the jury. Their argument was that he was wrong to say that they had to have reasonable grounds for their belief. The court of appeal supported the trial judge but gave leave to appeal to the House of Lords because the question of law was of public importance. It was to be decided *'whether in rape the defendant can properly be convicted notwithstanding that he, in fact, believed that the woman consented if such a belief was not based on reasonable grounds'* (Toner 1982 p132).

The Lords held that the man should be acquitted of rape if he honestly believed she was consenting, even if such belief were unreasonable. They took the view that the trial judge had misdirected the jury and the three men were released. This led a great amount of public protest which was aggravated by the fact that Lord Hailsham was attributed with the comment that it was commonly known that women often said 'no' when they meant 'yes' (Toner 1982 p134).

Following the case the Sexual Offenses Amendment Act 1976 was passed. It stated:

A man commits rape if:

(a) he has unlawful sexual intercourse with a woman who at the time of the intercourse does not consent to it; and

(b) at that time knows that she does not consent to the intercourse or he is reckless as to whether she consents to it.

Marital Rape

Until recently a husband could be held liable to charges of assault if he uses excessive force in his sexual activity or he could be charged with indecent assault for an act such as fellatio with which the wife had not consented. However, he could not otherwise be charged with the crime of rape. This exemption was derived from the common law position which was that a wife had agreed to sexual demands made by her husband by virtue of the marriage itself (Dewar 1989 p45). This decision was narrowed by a series of cases which established that a husband could be charged with rape if there were:
* a decree nisi of divorce (R v O'brien 1974),
* a judicial separation (R v Clarke 1949),
* a separation agreement (R v Roberts 1986),
* a non molestation or a personal protection order (R v Steel 1976)
* where he forced his wife to have intercourse with a third party
    (R v Cogan, R v Leak (1976).

However, Dewar wrote in 1989:

'It nevertheless remains the case that the existence of the exemption implies that there is a hierarchy of dominance and submission in marriage (Dewar 1989 p 45).

In 1985 the Fifteenth Report on Sexual Offenses. The Criminal Law Revision Committee decided against abolishing the exemption for a number of reasons including the argument that by including marital rape within the overall definition of the offence would diminish the offence of rape. For marital rape does not share the 'particularly grave' circumstances usually occurring in other cases of rape. If husbands were treated leniently it might lead to more lenient sentences for all rapists (Dewar 1989 p45). Furthermore it was proposed that police involvement might prevent a reconciliation. Some members of the committee argued that the law should stay out of the marital bed except when injury occurs. It did, however, unanimously agree that the exemption should be removed when a couple had ceased to cohabit (Dewar 1989 p46).

Rape and prostitutes

On 19th March 1996 a married businessman was sentenced to four years in gaol for raping five prostitutes. Concerned with the necessity for safe sex they had all insisted that the man should wear a condom. However, he refused and when they withdrew their agreement he raped them (Dyer 1996 p1). Mr Justice Latham commented:

'That is as much rape as if you had sexual intercourse with any other girl or woman without their consent'.

He continued to say that he imposed a relatively lenient sentence because the offenses were six years old and there was no evidence the man was a danger to other women (Dyer 1996 p1).

Sarah Maguire. a barrister and chairwoman of Rights of Women commented:

We applaud the judge's comments that women working as prostitutes have the same rights under law as any other women and they don't lose those rights because they sell sex. Selling sex to some men does not mean their bodies are available to all men on any terms they choose'.

The character of Convicted Rapists

In 1990 Diane Scully published 'Understanding sexual violence' in which she carried out interviews with 114 convicted rapists together with a control group of 75 other felons who had no such conviction. The sentences of the men in the study ranged from 10 years to seven life sentences plus 380 years. In the sample 46 per cent were white and 54 per cent were black. Just under half were married or cohabiting. Most of the men were from a working class background, but Scully suggests that this may well be more a reflection of the way the legal system works rather than which groups in society commit rape.

Men at the low end of the class scale are less able to afford sophisticated defense attorneys who specialise in beating rape charges (Scully 1990 p65).

In her sample 34 per cent of the rapists and 32 per cent of other felons reported that they had been victims of physical abuse. Furthermore, 9 per cent of rapists and 7 per cent of other felons said that they had been sexually abused as children (1990 p69).

The men in both her samples showed evidence of violence. Over half (55%) of rapists and over two thirds of other felons (68%) admitted having hit their significant woman at least once (Scully 1990 p72).

There was also evidence that the rapists committed other crimes. So 52 per cent of rapists and 39 per cent of other criminals had been arrested before by the age of fifteen. In all 84% of the rapists and 97% of the other felons had been arrested for one non sexual offense before their conviction (Scully 1992 p77). Only 37 per cent of rapists compared to 68 per cent of other felons had, however, been in prison for any reason prior to their current sentence (Scully 1990 p77). Almost two thirds of both groups felt that a woman should not move out of the house if her husband hit her and 45 per cent of the rapists and 40 per cent of the other felons agreed that women liked to be hit because they believe it means men care for them (Scully 1990 p85).

Scully reported the comment of a 34 year old man who threatened a fifteen year old girl walking on a beach with a knife. He told her:

A man's body is like a coke bottle, shake it up, put your thumb over the opening and feel the tension. When you take a woman out, woo her, then she says 'no, I'm a nice girl,' you have to use force. All men do this. She said 'no' but it was a societal 'no', she wanted to be coaxed. All women say 'no' when they mean 'yes' but it's a societal 'no' so they won't have to feel responsible later (Scully 1990 p104).

She said that amongst her sample many of the men reported that the lack of fierce resistance from the woman, even in the face of a weapon, still meant the act was not rape (1990 p105). She argued that many men were not capable of understanding the meaning of sexual violence to women. Others, however, believed the crime was such a moral outrage that it was beyond forgiveness:

I'm in here for rape and in my own mind, its the most disgusting crime, sickening. When people see me and know, I get sick (Scully 1990 p120).

<u>Why rape has increased in recent years?</u>

The increase in rape since 1979 has been considerable. There will be apologists who will point to the fact that it is less traumatic these days to report the crime. The fact that it is known that there are special sympathetic units to deal with cases of rape means that women are more likely to place their complaint. This may be partially true, however, it would be unrealistic to put more than a small part of the increase down to this factor.

<u>Rape of men</u> In recent years there have been a few reported cases of men being attacked in London. This does, however, seem relatively rare under usual social conditions and physical strength is clearly one factor.

In his study of Pentonville prison Terrence Morris reported that some normally heterorsexual men engaged in homosexual practices

145

for their period in custody. Rape may sometimes occur within this situation. However, it does seem far more in common in prisons in the US which may in part be due to the fact that prisoners in the United States are allowed far more freedom to move around. In Britain prisoners are much more likely to be restricted to their cells for the large part of the time.

The group 'Stop Prisoner Rape' is based in New York City and has produced a pamphlet **Hooking up: Protective Paring for Punks**. Part of it read.

'Many prisoners who have been raped by fellow inmates or who have been threatened with rape decide to become "hooked up" with another prisoner. However, distasteful the idea may seem, they believe it is the least damaging way to survive in custody. In most arrangements, the junior partner- in prison terms the "catcher" or "punk"-gives up his independence and control over his body to a senior partner-the "jocker", "man", "pitched" or "daddy"- in exchange for protection from violence and sexual assaults of other prisoners. This arrangement is preferable to a series of gang rapes (Sheffield 1996).'

Rape within US prisons is aa great worry for the inmates. One ex convict told me how he avoided it. *'The first time I went to the shower I took a shaarped pencil with me. When first man came in I pointed it into his neck and told him he would be dead if he tried anything.'* He said that worked for him, however, in a gang rape situation there is little that the individual could do.

How to reduce rape

There are no developed societies where rape does not occur but we have seen wide differences between countries and between areas of countries. So it should be possible to change the social conditions to become nearer to those of the societies with low rates of rape.

a <u>Reduce violence</u>

We have seen that rape is linked to violent activity and so any reduction in the overall rate of violence will reduce the rates of rape.

b <u>Move towards greater equality</u>

Unequal societies tend to produce people who have less stake in the overall society. By promoting equality we will be creating a more unified society. We shall see that one problem that could develop is that of an underclass where the usual values of society do not apply.

c <u>Police action</u>

Briere and Malamuth asked men whether they would be likely to rape if they could be assured that they would not be caught. They found that in a sample of 386 college men, 28% indicated some likelihood of both raping women and using force, 30 per cent would use force but not rape, 6 per cent would rape but not use force and only 40 per cent would not use either. This is a worrying finding and one would hope that in the future we would be socialising our men in a different way. However, it is clear that sympathetic police action will be needed in order to protect women.

d <u>Develop relationships</u>

If the two sexes relate together more on the basis of equality then the male pursuer/ female pursued dichotomy could be very much reduced even if not eliminated. If the sexes related to each other first as people then it is likely that the rates of rape would fall. This would happen especially if men and women began to seek other things from a relationship-such as companionship, working together and discussing other factors. This could lead to sex become less of an issue.

Research indicates that people with traditional attitudes towards the sex roles are more harsh on the victim and more lenient on the offender in comparison to people who believe in more equal sex roles (Scully 1990 p86)

Chapter 9

The relationship between poverty and crime.

The early theorists

The early criminologists argued quite strongly that poverty was a cause of crime. In his classic work on delinquency, Burt in 1925 drew attention to the fact that crime was concentrated in the poor areas.

The broad association between crime in the young and poverty in the home and its surroundings, is at once impressed upon the eye, if a chart be made of the distribution of juvenile delinquency in the different parts of London. With this aim in view I have secured the address of every boy and girl reported as an industrial school case during the last two years, namely, 1922 and 1923; and have calculated, for each electoral area in the country, what is the ratio of reported cases to the total number of children on the rolls of the Council's schools. The percentages so obtained have been made the basis of a map of juvenile crime. Such a map may be instructively compared with the map of London poverty published by Charles Booth (1925 pp70-1).'

The reference to Booth was of his report <u>Life and Labour in London</u> published in 1891. The highest rates of crime were on the three boroughs just north of the city- Holborn, Finsbury and Shoreditch.

Burt realised that many children of middle class parents committed crimes but were not prosecuted. In this respect he included a comment from W Clark-Hall:

'Those to whom philanthropic agencies or better-class parents bring cases direct for advice, without the intervention of the police, are amazed to find what numbers of young people commit offenses,

149

often serious and repeated, and yet, whether from accident or design, are never brought before a court' (1925 p21n)

However, despite the fact that the measured difference in crime levels was in part due the lack of police action, he also argued that those living in poverty were more likely to commit crime.

One factor to which he drew attention was the environment and the fact of poverty with 16% of people being below subsistence level (1925 p66). He was very clear about the way that the conditions of the poor could lead them into poverty:

'Of the various ways in which economic hardship may promote or encourage crime, the most immediate is through semi starvation. Hunger is the stimulus; and the ensuing crime is theft' (1925 p78).

He gave the example of two orphan brothers who stole for food. He said *'the raids and petty robberies of this diminutive pair sprang solely from hunger.* A sympathetic friend sent the two boys to a country home, and as soon as they were well fed all pilfering ceased (1925 p82). Although Burt regarded poverty as a source of crime he also noted other factors such as overcrowding and defective family relationships with those children.

In the United States during the 1920s a group of sociologists came up with similar findings to Burt which were later to be known as the Chicago school. Clifford Shaw and Henry McKay drew five circles on a map of Chicago to represent two mile intervals from the central business centre. They analysed the crime rate and found that it steadily decreased as one moved from the centre (Zone 1) to the outside (Zone 5). They noted that the delinquency rate was correlated with income as it rose steadily from zone one to zone five. However, overall their explanation of crime was more in terms of the social disorganisation in the central areas than poverty.

British criminologists

Terence Morris in a study of Croydon published in 1957 found similarly that certain areas had more crime. The highest rates were on identifiable housing estates which contained a high proportion of semi-skilled and unskilled workers. Also the council had a policy of placing 'problem' families, who, for example, did not pay their rent, on these estates. The children of these families had much higher crime rates than usual. However, Morris found that the areas had close knit communities with little evidence of social disorganisation. He did not regard the high crime level in these areas as a 'natural development' because in part it had to do with political decisions.

Wilson considered high crime areas in Bristol and proposed that councils did not intentionally create problem areas. However, he suggested that in order to reduce likely deficits some families were offered housing with low rents. This led in due course to other people avoiding such areas and caused a cycle as the better off avoided such areas and so they could only be let to other 'problem' families. So there was a cycle of deprivation.

David Downes in **'The Delinquent Solution'** drew attention to the lack of opportunities for working class youths in the areas of Stepny and Poplar. As discussed in Chapter Three he suggested that improved education and facilities would reduce the level of juvenile crime.

Lea and Young pointed out that it is much too simplistic to say that poverty causes crime. They said there is a great amount of middle class crime carried out by wealthy executives. They also suggested that even when controlling for the degree of poverty within the poorest groups there are wide variations. They quoted the work of Charles Silberman who found that in Texas, African-Americans were about as poor as Mexican-Americans but were four times as likely to be in prison for a felony. In San Diego 1971-3 African

Americans were seven times as likely to be arrested for homicide, over four times as likely to be arrested for rape and almost eight times as likely to be arrested for robbery in comparison Mexican-Americans. In New York the Puerto Ricans had a median income 20% below that of the African Americans and yet hispanics had only one third the arrest rate for violent crime (1993 p86).

They argued that black Americans have had a much different experience of discrimination compared to Hispanics and quoted Silberman:

When one reflects the history of black people in this country, what is remarkable is not how much, but how little black violence there has always been. Certainly, it would be hard to imagine an environment better calculated to evoke violence than the one in which black Americans have lived (Lea and Young 1993 p87-8).

They continued to argue that it is not absolute poverty but rather poverty which is seen to be unfair, which creates discontent. So relative deprivation is important and where the discontent has no political solution it leads to crime. They commented:

The equation is simple: relative deprivation equals discontent; discontent plus lack of political solution equals crime (1993 p88).

This analysis is very important to begin discussing the effects of inequality since the second World War and especially since 1979.

The growth in poverty

In the early 1960s there were many who believed that there was a gradual movement towards equality. This was challenged by Richard Titmuss when writing a new introduction to Tawney's 'Equality'. He pointed out that the move towards equality occurred during the Second World War and that there was no necessary trend. At this time the philosophy of the Conservative Party was well to the left of what it became from 1979. Harold MacMillan talked of the need for full employment and the Welfare State. In 1938 in his book <u>The Middle Way</u> he called for the nationalisation of the coal industry and a subsequent Conservative Prime Minister, Ted Heath, actually nationalised Rolls Royce. However, with the following of new right policies in the 1980s and 1990s inequalities increased.

The ideas behind the growth in inequality

There is no doubt that ideas of the self styled 'new right' underlay much of the policy of the British Government during the period 1979-1995. The back cover of the paperback edition of the book **Free to Choose** by M and R Friedman quotes the Observer:

'With unabashed monetarists in Downing Street....Milton Friedman now has a chance to see if a Government acknowledging his influence can put principle into practice.'

Since then we have seen the wholesale privatisation of industry. The new right philosophy also explains some rather unusual statements such as Mrs Thatcher's claim that:

'There is no such thing as society. There are individual men and women and there are families. And no government can do anything except through people and people must look after themselves first' (Thatcher 1995 p626).

In this comment she was following the general theme of the argument advanced by the new right in proposition 2 below. The argument underlying the views of the New Right as set out for popular consumption by the Friedmans can be summed up as a number of propositions.

1 Modern economics can be traced back to the ideas of Adam Smith and the **Wealth of Nations** which analysed the way in which

a market system could combine the freedom of individuals to pursue their own objectives with the extensive co-operation to produce their needs (1980 p20).

2 The greatest good for society is produced by individuals working for the benefit of themselves and their families. Each person working for his/her own interests serves the interests of the society (1980 p32).

3 If an exchange between two people is voluntary it will not occur unless both believe they will benefit. A free market presents an 'invisible hand' in such a way as to make everybody better off (1980 pp 20, 31).

4 Governments have a tendency to grow and interfere with the freedom of individuals. This should be resisted. One problem is that when people are spending the money of others they are not so careful as when they are spending money on behalf of themselves. (1980 p146).

5 Having resources owned by the Government is negative because *when everybody owns something, nobody owns it, and nobody has a direct interest in maintaining or improving its condition.'* (1980 p43)

6 The role of Government should be limited but it should have four roles-the first three come directly from Adam Smith. They are to protect society from violence and invasion, to protect members of society from injustice or oppression, and to maintain certain public works. To these three the Friedman's believe a fourth needs to be added which is to protect individuals who cannot be regarded as 'responsible' (1980 pp52-54). These roles although necessary are open to abuse and so a watchful eye should be kept.

7 One of the reasons for a limited role for Government is that private enterprise is more efficient (1980 p144).

8 Unions and such organisations as the Professional Associations restrict entry in order to obtain higher incomes. In so doing they aim to restrict the opportunities of others. A free market in contrast will create benefits for all.

9 Any movement towards reducing inequality will lead to a stifling of initiative, an increase in bureaucracy and a reduction of economic growth. A country that puts equality ahead of freedom will end up neither equal nor free (1980 p177).

These ideas underpinned much of the policy of the British Government during the period 1979-1995. However, there are several problems with the effects of this theory. The first is that it leads there to be winners and losers. Robert Wharton a business consultant with one of the major City firms commented: *The New right theorists believe that everyone will be a winner. However, history shows that to be a mistaken belief' (personal communication June 1995).*

Evidence for the Growth in inequality

There have been a number of reports documenting the growth of inequality since 1979. A major report from the Joseph Rowntree Foundation considered the changes in income for the period 1961-1991 and was based on a detailed examination of the data of 200,000 households (Goodman and Webb 1994 p1). In order to compare the relative income of one household against another it is clear that what is important is not total income of the family but also the number of people it has to support, how many of these are children and what age they are. Young children need less income than older ones. So the report used 'equivalence scales' with a childless couple counting as 1.0, a single person as 0.61 and a couple with two children aged 11 years and 4 years having an equivalence of 1.43. One way of interpreting this is to say that a single person needs 61% of that of a childless couple to attain the same living standard (Goodman and Webb p5). Income is net of income taxes, National Insurance contributions and local taxes.

The report aimed to produce and analysis of trends in poverty, inequality and real living standards during the period. There are at least two possible measures. One is income before housing costs (BHC) and the other is income after housing costs (AHC). In some sense it might seem that income after housing costs is a more appropriate measure because if rents rise and there are no other changes then this means that the overall disposable income will inevitably fall. However, for some families a rise in housing costs could be because they have moved into better accommodation. For example a young couple may have moved out of rented accommodation into owner occupation and will regard this as progress. Refer Table 9.1

Percentage of income as a measure of inequality

A second way of considering income inequality is by considering the percentage of income owned by the different segments of the population. For example the bottom tenth of the population held 41/2% of total income in 1961 but it had dropped to 3% by 1991.

This is made clearer by considering the relationship between the income of the top and bottom ten per cent of the society. The rise in inequality shows clearly with the ratio rising from just over three times to over four times. The inequality becomes more pronounced after housing costs are taken into account. To quote the Nuffield report:

Taking into account the effects of housing costs can greatly affect assessment of changes in real living standards. The real incomes of the poorest tenth ranked by income after housing costs actually fell sharply from a peak in 1979 of £73 per week to just over £61 per week in 1991 (both in 1994 prices). This represented a return of living standards of a quarter of a century ago, although the most recent figures have been strongly affected by a growth in low income self employment and should be treated with some caution (1994 p66).

Another piece of research showed that while the richest 10% of the population gained £87 a week from tax cuts and shifts to direct taxation the poorest 10% lost £1 a week (Oppenheim 1993). An official report from the Department of Social Security showed that when housing costs were taken into account the poorest 10% of the population suffered a 14% loss in real income between 1979 and 1990-1. In contrast the richest fifth of the population had over a 20% rise. (DSS 1993) A striking figure that shows the increase in inequality is that in 1979 only 9% of people had incomes less than half the national average. This figure rose to 25% by 1990-93 (DSS 1993). There was also a great increase in the number of individuals with below 50% of average income. The numbers increased from four million to over ten million. There was a reduction in the real value of social security benefits leading to the unemployed becoming worse off (Goodman and Webb 1994 p35).

Who are the poor?

Although we have seen a rise in the number of poor, the question arises as to which group they belong. In the popular mythology of traditional marriage there was the man who was the 'breadwinner' with the woman being at home in charge of the domestic arrangements. Many Conservatives wanted to return to that however, the changes were in a totally opposite direction.

*   The unemployed. The percentage of men in full time employment fell. Between 1971 and 1991 the proportion of working age men in full time employment fell by almost a fifth (DSS 1993 p42).

* Rising number of divorced and never married mothers. Not all of these would be outside relationships and there has been an

increase in the percentage of births outside marriage where two partners registered the birth. However, many of these mothers have limited financial support.

* Increasing number of married/attached men on low wages. This means that when they have children and their wife or partner has to stop work they rapidly descend into poverty.

* Families with children have become relatively worse off compared to childless families (DSS 1993 P38). This has consistently been the case. It was in large part due to a number of measures taken against children by the Government.

1 Freezing of child support. This was the case for most of the Thatcher years.

2 Removal of maternity benefits. In 1987 the Government removed universal maternity benefits and argued that they were going to target them upon the most needy. The maternity grant was increased from £80 to £100 in April 1990 but then was frozen and was still £100 in April 1996.

3 Removing tax concessions of children.

The fact that people with children are so financially disadvantaged compared to the rest of society is a problem. Very often people have to drop from two incomes to one at a time when they have to be moving to larger houses or flats in order to create the extra room needed. The general disadvantage of families means that children are more likely to be raised in poverty and so face the relative deprivation which is one factor in crime.

The society could take the view that those people raising children are performing a difficult if rewarding task on behalf of everyone. They could then be viewed far more positively and by means of tax concessions, child allowances and maternity grants be helped to provide their children with a good quality of life.

We can concur with the comments of Richard Wilkinson:

For the sake of the economy and society as a whole, as well as young people themselves, we need greater investment in human capital. While children's charities such as Barnado's do their best to put young lives together, action to remove relative poverty is a priority if we are to prevent them from being torn apart in the first place (1994 pvii).

The unemployed

Observers have noted that unemployment came to become an important part of the poorest groups as early as the late 1960s but that it increased in importance in the late 1970s and 1980's (Goodman and Webb 1994 p41)

Lone parent households

Around one in six children is now in a one parent household (Goodman and Webb p42). The percentage of births outside marriage rose from 8 per cent in 1970 to 12 per cent in 1980 and 30 per cent in 1990. Although Burghes points out that the percentage of all families with dependent children has only fallen from 92% in 1971 to 81 per cent in 1991 (1993). This may have an important impact on crime rates.

One factor is that fathers in such circumstances may not play so important a role in their children's lives. Many lose touch either through a wish to avoid paying maintenance or through denial of access. Some wealthy men may behave like the former Conservative Minister Cecil Parkinson and provide financially help but not play any proper role in their children's lives and leave the caring role to others.

In Chapter four we discussed the argument promoted by right wing sociologists that the breakdown of the traditional nuclear family leads to social dislocation and crime (Dennis 1993, Morgan 1995). However, Wilkinson rightly points out that the proportion of married and cohabiting couples only fell from 92% in 1971 to 81% in 1991 and so this was unlikely to be the total explanation. Furthermore, as mentioned earlier international comparisons show that Japan and Sweden are first and second in the international league tables of health and have low crime rates. However, while Japan comes close to the traditional model of a nuclear family with low births outside marriage and low divorce rates, Sweden is only surpassed by Iceland in the degree of its departure from the nuclear model. Wilkinson continues to argue:

'One of the reasons that single parents in Sweden are able to maintain good health figures is that only two per cent of Swedish children in lone parent families were in relative poverty contrasted to an average of 21% for a group of eight countries in the OECD.' (Wilkinson 1994 p 11).

This evidence suggests it is not one parent families that are the problem so much as that they are often in poverty. This suggestion is lent support by Scully who said that if a female dominated head were so problematical we would expect high levels of violence in traditional female dominated societies (1990 p66).

Housing, homelessness and poverty

Housing stock has suffered from the move to the right. Iona Heath argues that social housing in Britain has a one hundred and fifty year history of effectiveness as a health intervention. She points out that until 1951 central government's responsibility for health was placed within the Ministry of Health (1994 p1675).

In contrast Government spending on housing fell from £13.1 billion in 1979 to £5.8 billion in 1992, while the sale of public housing realised $28 billion by the end of 1993. Shelter pointed out that the number of homeless people more than doubled between 1978 and 1989 when it was 126,680. In 1993 the figure had increased further to 139,110 (Shelter 1990 and 1995). The 1991 census identified 2,827 rough sleepers and 19,417 hostel dwellers, although these are thought to be gross underestimates. In inner city wards it was calculated that 30% of young men had not been included in the census (Brown 1995). It is therefore not surprising that Homeless Network, estimated that 3,000 people spent all or part of 1994 sleeping on London's streets (Heath 1994 p1675).

One factor related to homelessness for young people is that in 1988 benefit rates were reduced for 18-24 year olds and general entitlement to income support was removed for most unemployed 16 and 17 year olds. In 1991 the Government commissioned a survey of 16 and 17 year olds who had claimed special hardship allowance. There were 76,957 such claims in the first nine months of 1992. The children's charity Dr Barnado's published evidence commenting that these young people presented a sorry state:

'45% had been forced to sleep "rough" at some point, many were still homeless, half had no money, and a quarter of them said they had needed to beg, steal or sell drugs in order to survive. A quarter already had criminal convictions, and a quarter of the girls were pregnant.'

Overall Heath comments:

'The consequent fall in the quantity and quality of local authority housing has led to growing social, economic and health disparities between local authority tenants and home owners...the lack of investment in decent affordable housing produces and sustains homelessness, which in turn damages health, increases the demand for health care, increases the costs of health care.'
(1994 p1676).

So homelessness is a continuing problem and young people with such experience are clearly at more risk of suffering from crime and may well be more likely to commit it. Prison may be a welcome improvement in living conditions for some people.

Other evidence on the growth in inequality In October 1995 there was further evidence of the worsening position of Britain compared to the rest of the world. Richard Thomas in an article entitled 'UK worst in rich and poor divide' reported that in the 1980s the gap between the rich and poor grew faster in England and Wales than any other industrialised country.

The study, commissioned by the free market Organisation for Economic Co-operation and Development showed that the United States was the most unequal country in the developed world but that Britain had been catching up. At the start of the first Thatcher administration the richest one in five of the population had 36 per cent of the income. At the end of the decade it had risen to 43 per cent.

An official study showed that after housing costs had been taken into account the group having the lowest 10% of income suffered a 14% decline in real income. In contrast while the top 10% had a rise of over 20% due in part to a move away from direct to indirect taxation. So, whereas in 1979 only 9% of the population received less than 50% of average income, the proportion had risen to 24% by 1990-3 (Department of Social Security 1993) Similar evidence came from Wilkinson. He reported in 1983 The ratio of the income of the richest 20% to the poorest 20% was 4.0. It grew with an especially steep rise between 1895-7 until in 1991 the ratio was over 5.7. (Wilkinson 1994p4) During this period there was also evidence of an increase in crime rates and total reported increase of 80% and of violent crime 90% during the period. (Wilkinson 1994 p1)

A study in the Northern region showed that between 1981-1991 there were large increases in mortality differences between the most deprived and most affluent electoral wards. (Phillimore and Beattie 1993) Similarly, Glasgow which contains 80% of the most deprived postcode sectors in Scotland has shown a worsening of mortality compared to the rest of Scotland. (Forwell 1993) So it seems clear that when the more detailed analysis is completed it will reveal greater social class differences than in the past and an increase in relative deprivation and crime that could have been avoided by reducing class differences.

Inequality health and crime.

In 1980 income inequalities between Britain and Japan were similar. Since that time Japan's inequality has declined to become the lowest of any country reporting to the World Bank. In contrast Britain's inequalities have increased (Wilkinson 1994 p22). In fact a report by the Joseph Rowntree Foundation in February 1995 found that in Britain the gap between the rich and the poor was the widest since the war and that since 1977 the number of people with less than half the national average had trebled. Britain's inequality had grown faster than any other comparative country. The report called for collective investment to be placed before tax cuts. (Hutton 1995 p7)

In some other countries inequalities have narrowed. This applies to Spain, Ireland, Denmark and Italy (Hutton 1995 p7). In these countries crime rates will probably reduce. In contrast in Britain both inequalities and crime rates have increased. When data is published in future years there is little doubt that the differences will be accentuated.(Wilkinson 1994 p22).

From a series of studies there is evidence that inequality is not only linked to crime but also to health (Townsend 1992, Whitehead 1992, Wilkinson 1994). In Britain in the 1970s and 1980s unskilled manual workers were found to have twice the death rates found amongst those in professional occupations and their families (Whitehead 1992). Commenting on the data Wilkinson suggests that the social class differences in death rates are not fixed nor unalterable (1994 p16).

More recent trends in the privatisation of industry and increased salaries for the leaders of the companies have created high profile differences between groups. At the end of 1994 British Gas reported a 75% increase in salary for its chief executive to £475,000 while at about the same time it cut the wages of its workforce and in the words of a quality newspaper 'slashed the pipeline safety budget'(Rose 1994). Writing in the BMJ at the end of 1994 Peter Towsend commented:

'This year has seen recurring reports of the swelling salaries and breathtaking pronouncements of rich people. Early this month Iain Valance, the chairman of British Telecom, described his salary- which with additions, is now in excess of £750,000, as 'modest'. By comparison with what is going on at the top of Britain's hierarchy in the 75 largest non financial companies perhaps he was right.' (Townsend 1994 p1674)

He continued to note that inequality had not only increased but there was a tendency for certain members of the Government to stigmatise the poor, rather than help them as in the past. A comment by Peter Lilley that young ladies get pregnant to jump the housing list was seen is typical of a comment made which has little relevance to young mothers. We have seen that three quarters of them live with their parents.

A study in 350 families in 1991 found that two thirds of low income families found it was difficult to afford a healthy diet for their children. Nearly half of all parents said they had gone hungry in the past year in order to make sure other family members had adequate food. One in ten children under five had gone without

164

food in the previous month, and two thirds of the children and over half the parents were eating poor diets. (National Children's Homes 1991). Other research for the National Children's Home charity calculated that the basic social security benefit paid to more than 1.5 million families was only £5.46 a week. At this level it was not enough to pay for the diet prescribed for a child in a Victorian workhouse. They costed diets for Bethnal Green in 1876 and for the Poor Law Orders in 1913 at £5.46 and £7.07 respectively. In 1913 the children had bread and milk for breakfast; beef, potatoes or vegetables and fresh fruit pudding for lunch; and supper of seed cake and cocoa. This diet is much better than can be afforded by Britain's poor today. Time White the charities chief executive commented *'It is appalling, as we approach the year 2000, that even an 1876 workhouse diet is too expensive for one in four of our children.'* (Brindle 1994 p5)

Wilkinson and inequality

I quoted Wilkinson above but it is worth considering his work in more detail. In an earlier work on economic growth we had argued that once countries had developed past a certain point a crucial factor was not further economic growth but rather the way money is spent within the society. So countries like the United States had worse health statistics than other countries like the Netherlands because it had a great amount of inequality and an underclass unable to share in the benefits of the society. (Francome and Wharton 1973, Francome 1990)

In a series of widely quoted articles dating back to 1986 Wilkinson has drawn attention to the adverse effects of inequality both on health and crime (1986, 1994). He sets out to answer the question as to why as society has become more prosperous materially has there been increasing signs of social failure. His general argument is similar to that advanced by Young and Lea and is that relative poverty 'is a much more destructive force than is generally recognised'(1994 pvii). He noted the generally increase in crime in

165

society as we outlined in chapter two and also he documented other forms of dislocation:

* There was between a four and five-fold increase in the number of deaths from solvent abuse between 1980 and 1990.

* The proportion of children on child protection registers almost quadrupled during the 1980s.

* The number of children in care rose from 1985 onwards.

* There was a dramatic increase in the proportion of children excluded from school.

* The suicide rate of young men aged 15-24 increased by 75% between 1983-1990 (1994 p1).

* The proportion of children living in relative poverty tripled during the 1980s. By the early 1990s almost one third of children came from homes below the EC relative poverty income poverty line ie their household had less than half the annual income (Wilkinson 1994 p31).

* There is a relationship between deprivation and unsocial behaviour. So the Child Development study which followed up 17,000 people born in 1958 found that those with socio-economic disadvantage were more predisposed to negative deviance. Those identified by teachers as 'deviant' using the Rutter Behaviourial Scale and having 'emotional or conduct disorders' also scored much less well in health measures even when taking other 'social and economic factors into account'(Wilkinson 1994 p31).

* There are tens of thousands of unemployed and aged 16 and 17 year olds who make claims for discretionary severe hardship allowance. Nearly half (45%) had been forced to sleep rough at some time (Wilkinson 1994 p36).

In the British Medical Journal in 1992 Wilkinson asserted that the international data showed that if Britain were to adopt policies leading to more equal income distribution similar to those of other European countries then about two years would be added to British life expectancy. It would also help with the crime situation because there is clearly a pattern between deprivation, poverty and crime.

Unfortunately there has been a great widening of income disparities. More recent developments since Wilkinson's work suggests that inequality will have increased further. For example the imposition of 8% VAT on fuel fell proportionately more heavily on the poor.

Data from eight OECD countries showed that The USA had the highest crime and infant mortality rates as well as the highest percentage in relative poverty. The UK had the second highest percentage in relative poverty and the third highest infant mortality rate after The United States and Canada. Sweden, Norway, Switzerland and the Netherlands had much lower infant mortality rates and much less relative poverty. (Wennemo 1993) One factor probably influencing the increase in crime in the United States is the growth in inequality during the 1970s and especially the 1980s as the country followed similar economic policies to Britain. Health was also affected and in the United States differences in life expectancy between white and black people increased with widening income differentials. (Davey Smith and Egger 1993)

Conclusion:

In this chapter we have shown the reasons behind the rise in inequality and documented its development. We have had an increase in relative poverty which leads to people not sharing the same values.

There has also been an increase in unemployment and in January 1996 Home Office researchers published a report based on 2,500 interviews which proposed that there was a link between crime and joblessness. This finding contradicted the governments assertions of their being no link between the two. The report argued that by the age of twenty five 30 per cent of young men were involved in some crime. It continued to say that the high level of unemployment was making it far more difficult for young delinquents to grow up and make the transition to responsible adulthood (Travis 1996).

So there is a need to move towards greater equality and to try and ensure that young people of all levels of intelligence have adult roles to move into so that they can fulfil their responsibilities.

Chapter 10

Prostitution-A Victimless Crime?

The headline in the Observer was the **Week when sex taboos came out** (4th August 1996 p3). The article continued to say that amongst other things such as the Barnet NHS Trust advertising for gay men to do aids prevention work, a chief constable had called for legalised brothels. Keith Hellawell said: *'We ought to have legally controlled brothels... to control prostitution for the females security'.*

In arguing this case a debate on prostitution that had been simmering for some time came out into the open. Historically society has had conflicting emotions when considering this issue.

'The oldest profession' has been seen by many as a grave threat to family life. Speck reports *'Several commentators in the early eighteenth century expressed concern that marriage was going out of fashion, especially in London. Some blamed it on the availability of whores, others on the expense of supporting a wife.' (1977* p63)

Blake suggests that prostitution may be compared with homosexuality in that it too may be seen as a threat. In this respect she quotes the functionalist sociologist Kingsley Davis:

Homosexual intercourse is obviously incompatible with the family and the sexual bargaining situation. The norms and attitudes required to support these institutions as a means of getting the business of reproduction and sexual allocation accomplished tend to downgrade homosexuality..(which) .. directly competes with male/female relationships (Blake 1974 p298).

She suggests that similar considerations apply to prostitution and that society derogates it to a pariah status in order to help channel sexual activity into the confines of marriage and parenthood.

Speaking of the condemnation of the prostitute, Kingsley Davis made a comment which also says a great deal about the traditional approach to marriage. He said:

Her willingness to sell her favours and her feeling of emotional indifference are also condemned but... a wife who submits dutifully but reluctantly to intercourse is often considered virtuous for that reason, although she is expected to cherish her husband in a spiritual sense. The trading of sexual favours for a consideration is what is done in a marriage, for in consenting to get married a woman exchanges her sexual favours for economic support. As long as the bargain struck is one that achieves a stable relationship, especially a marriage, the mores offer praise rather than condemnation for the trade. The prostitutes affront is that she trades promiscuously (Blake 1974 p298).

Under this view of marriage a man was supposed to be the breadwinner who would support his wife especially when she was vulnerable as during pregnancy and rearing small children. Part of the reward for this is to be looked after by the wife including a stable sexual relationship. Prostitution may be seen as a threat to marriage because it provides sex outside this system. Amongst single men it means that if they can get sex there may be less motivation to take on the necessary responsibilities of marriage. This is an argument against all premarital sex of course. In addition prostitution amongst married men means a diversion of finances away from the family and the possible introduction of venereal disease to innocent wives. So it is to be deprecated.

However, others have regarded prostitution more positively and so there has always been a strong ambivalence. Suppress prostitution wrote St Augustine, *'and capricious lusts will overthrow society'* (Salgado 1992 p39). More recently the sociologist Albert Cohen maintained that some kinds of deviance acted to protect society: *'prostitution performs such a safety valve function without threatening the institution of the family.'* In his view the prostitute provides extra or pre marital activity at a financial cost but not usually posing a strong emotional threat (Cohen 1966).

Prostitution in the past

Amongst the Romans there was a strong relationship between hot baths and bawdy houses. This relationship still continues in terms of saunas.

In Britain Salgado suggests, that at least until the sixteenth century Southwark was recognised as a place for fleshly pleasures and he commented:

The association of Southwark with pleasures of various kinds probably goes back to the time when the first Roman legions encamped there in AD 54 (1995 p37).

In 1162 the area was under control of the Bishop of Winchester and contained very many brothels and Henry 11 put forward his 'Ordinances touching upon the government of the stews of Southwark'. Originally a stew was a sweating or steam bath which was introduced by the Romans. The Bishop controlled the brothels and attempted to enforce certain rules such as that brothel keepers were not allowed to prevent the freedom of movement of single women or stop a woman from leaving prostitution. They were also not allowed to have married women or nuns on their staff. Southwark until 1550 was not part of London and was treated ambivalently by Londoners. There was a fascination for its pleasures but there was also a problem in that any wanted man could cross London Bridge to escape (Salgado 1995 p39).

In the early part of the sixteenth century brothels had to be painted white and to carry a distinctive sign on the most celebrated was called the Cardinal's Hat. The reason for this is not clear. However, Salgado suggests it was possibly *'not because of any particular ecclesiastical connection but because of association in colour and shape with the tip of the male sexual organ (Salgado 1995 p41).*

In 1546 Henry V111 ordered a ban on the brothels but this attempt at suppression ended with his death from syphilis in the following year. Under his son Edward V1 the brothels were re-opened together with their signs. During the reign of Elizabeth prostitution was illegal but still seems to have flourished (Salgado 1995 p41). A woman found guilty of prostitution might have her head shaved and be paraded through the streets with a paper on her forehead telling of her shame. Those running brothels tried to bribe the officials in money or with favour but if they failed they might also be prosecuted and given similar treatment to the prostitutes. There is plenty of evidence of prostitution during Elizabethan times. This was not only those born locally but also women who were mainly from the poorer classes who would go to London and find that this was a way of providing a better standard of living, despite the risks of violence and venereal disease.

There were often links between prostitutes and crime. Scams were sometimes arranged and one was for a 'wronged husband' to turn up and demand compensation (Salgado 1995 p53).

Laslet reports that prostitution was common in London from the sixteenth to the nineteenth centuries. Where very often a man of education and high social position often went with prostitutes from the lowest social level (Laslet 1983 p167).

Prostitution in the nineteenth century

A prostitute described her day to the researcher Bracebridge Hemyng;

If I have no letters or visits from any of my friends, I get up about four o'clock, dress and dine: after that I may walk about the streets for an hour or two and pick up anyone I am fortunate enough to

172

meet, that is if I want money; afterwards I go to the Holborn, dance a little, and if anyone likes me I take him home with me. If not I go to the Haymarket, and wander from one cafe to another, from Sally's to the Carlton, from Barns' to Sams', and if I find no one there I go, if I feel inclined, to the divans. I like the Grand Turkish best, but you don't as a rule find good men at any of the divans (Chesney 1970 p308).

It is widely recognised that during this period of time there was a great amount of prostitution. There are a number of reasons for this. Some of them relate to the increase in demand from the men and others rate to the supply of women to prostitution.

A) Trevelyan suggests that in the eighteenth century 'kept mistresses' were an important part of society. However, the growing respectability of the better off groups in society meant that such open adultery could not be tolerated. Consequently, the demand was diverted to the prostitute who could be visited in secret (1970 p504)

B) Another factor was proposed by Acton, a contemporary observer who trained as a doctor at the Female Venereal Hospital in Paris and worked in a public clinic in London. He said the Victorian fear of imprudent marriages resulting in a fall in standard of living led to single upper and middle class men having to wait until they were older and more established before they could marry. Others who were less well off might even have to decide not to wed. Both these groups of men would have some members who would decide to use the services of prostitutes.

C) Given the strictures of Victorian society, many of the men may well have found prostitutes attractive simply because it was much easier to go with such a woman and have an uncomplicated sexual relationship.

D) The fact that Britain was a seafaring nation increased the number of men who were without women for a long period of time and then who returned to port with money to spend.

E) The primary source of supply of prostitutes was undoubtedly poverty. Contemporary observers such as Acton were agreed that women were paid so little that they were driven to become prostitutes. Similarly Mayhew interviewed a number of London garment workers and found:

Many of them accepted whoring as an inescapable result of not having a man to help to support them. One girl was pregnant by a young artisan who had left her, and she confessed she was 'obligated to go a bad way' to live. In busy times she managed to stitch a dozen pairs of trousers a week at seven or eight pence apiece; but thread and lighting had to be paid for and, since work was irregular, she cleared on average no more than three shillings a week. Yet trouser-making was relatively well paid. 'There isn't,' she said 'one young girl as can get her living by slop work': only those whose parents kept them in food and shelter could afford to remain virtuous (Chesney 1970 p312-3).

Mayhew carried out a small survey of the women and interviewed them all separately before concluding that one in four earned extra money by prostitution.

F) The movement to the towns was important and the traditional restraints of the countryside for the need to maintain a 'good name' did not apply.

G) Another factor relating to the supply of women is put down by Trevelyan to the *'harshness of the worlds ethical code, which many parents endorsed, too often drove a girl once seduced to prostitution. (1970 p504)'*. For many people any woman who had once broken the strict rules of chastity was a 'fallen woman' and more or less placed on a par with the prostitute.

H) 'Dollymops' were a source of recruits for prostitution according to Chesney (1970 p324). This might be a young milliner's or dressmaker's assistant who lived away from the premises. Or a young nursemaid taking a child out to the park. She was an attractive young female and *'the essential thing was that she was an attractive working girl not under constant supervision who flirted with men and eventually went to bed with them, either for fun or gain or both at once'* (1970 p324).

<u>Nasty, brutish and short</u> There were many who believed that the prostitutes life would be short. However, Acton took the view that many women who were prostitutes would in fact return to 'normal' society:

Acton had 'every reason to believe, that by far the larger number of women who have resorted to prostitution, for a livelihood, return sooner or later to a more regular course of life.' Many were on the look out for making a 'dash at respectability' through marriage, and to a most surprising and year by year 'increasing extent' they succeeded. (Chesney 1970 p317-8).

There were several particularly unfortunate problems associated with victorian prostitution. The first is the use of young girls for prostitution. Sexual intercourse was proscribed with girls under the age of twelve. However, this was often not enforced (Chesney 1970 p325). Acton said that the sight of young prostitutes following men was the cause of much foreign comment.

Secondly, the use of young virgins was made worse by the alleged belief that intercourse with a virgin was seen as a cure for venereal disease. If prostitutes became ill it was often very difficult for them to get relief as the poor law officials would make it very difficult. In fact it is suggested that some prostitutes sometimes obtained treatment by becoming jailed (Chesney 1970 p356).

175

One of the reasons for the open character of prostitution during the nineteenth century was the 1851 Common Lodging House Act. Until that point a number of prostitutes would club together to rent a room. However, this act gave the police the right to inspect any common lodging house (Chesney 1970 p357). In 1864 the first Contagious Diseases Act was passed, providing in some cases for the inspection of women suspected of passing on venereal disease and in 1866 prostitutes at various ports became subject to periodic medical checks. In 1869 further enactments made every prostitute subject to fortnightly examination if she worked within fifteen miles of major garrison towns except London (Chesney 1970 p359). The laws were very sexist in that the did not apply to men and were also oppressive. Women in the areas were asked to sign a voluntary submission' and then to be inspected. It was not so voluntary, however, for if the woman refused to sign she would be taken in front of the magistrates and had to prove that she led a virtuous life. If she could not do so she was liable to imprisonment.

The opposition to the laws was led by Josephine Butler and in this matter she was supported by her clergyman husband. She argued that it was a disgrace that women should be seduced by men and then punished for it by the state while the man went free. Further, in order to appeal to Victorian delicacy, she drew attention to the affront to modesty of the compulsory vaginal examination. When a by election occurred in Colchester she helped bring down the Liberal candidate who was a supporter of the Acts. They were suspended in 1883 and repealed three years later. In the campaign of opposition they brought up a number of other issues such as the fate of the so called 'fallen women'. This pressure led to the 1885 Criminal Law Amendment Act. This statute made it easier to prosecute brothel keepers as the previous legal defences were dismantled. The brothel keepers could be fined and sentenced to three months imprisonment for the first offence. Much heavier penalties could be imposed on those found guilty of procuring young women for prostitution. So 1885 marked the end of a period of openness of prostitution and of course homosexuality too.

It seemed that prostitution declined after the first world war. this was probably the case in both in Britain and the United States. In the USA Judge Ben Lindsey stressed the fact that before the war he had talked to a hundred boys and half admitted they had been with prostitutes in the red light district. However, since the war there had been a relaxation of sexual morals and so the young men were now turning to girls in their own class (Francome 1984 p54).

The Wolfendon report on Homosexual Offenses and Prostitution was published in 1957. This proposed three changes. First that there should be a distinction between law and morality, so prostitution may be immoral but that did not mean that the law needed to be involved. Secondly, there should be an attempt to rationalise resources towards prostitution whilst increasing the number of convictions. Thirdly it aimed to change police practices in order to make prostitution less visible (Matthews 1986 p189). The aim was, therefore, to reduce the role of law so that it was only involved with the activities of prostitutes which offended the public citizen or which were related to exploitation of others (Wolfendon 1957 p80). The Street Offenses Act 1959 proved extremely successful in removing prostitution from view. The Working Party on Vagrancy and Street Offenses argued that the Street Offenses Act was meeting the objectives of the Woldendon Committee. There was a change in practice in 1983 when imprisonment was removed as a method of punishment. However, as Matthews pointed out there was a simultaneous rise in the number of prosecutions for soliciting. These rose from 6,000 in 1982 to around 10,000 in 1983 and increased so that increasing numbers of prostitutes were sent to prison for non payment of fines (1986 p191).

There were, however objections to the law from various feminist organisations. One of the problems was the fact that a woman who was designated a 'common prostitute' was assumed by the courts to be guilty and to be able to be convicted on police evidence alone. There is no such concept as a 'common john' and so this double standard affronts notions of equality. The law also provides the police with a large amount of discretion and the consequent possibilities of corruption (Matthews 1986 p190).

In the United States such groups as COYOTE (Call of your old Tired Ethics) have challenged prostitution laws on the grounds that they infringe civil liberties and rights of privacy. One of the criticisms is that vacancy type laws used to control so called 'disorderly persons' arrest people on the basis of their 'type' rather than specific acts they have committed.

Why women become prostitutes

The BMJ reported a study at the Glasgow Drop-in Centre which was a health care and social work for female prostitutes. Over four nights in August 1992 they invited 52 women attending sequentially to participate in a survey and all but one did so. Of the 51 participants 44 (86%) were injecting drug users. They were aged between 17 and 62 years with a median age of around 25 years. (Carr, Goldberg and Green 1994 p538). Other factors are linked to poverty. The Observer reported that one part time prostitute is 45 year old woman with a disabled daughter whose husband is serving a life sentence. She cannot afford to live on benefits and so supplements her income (Mellor 1996)

Men and criminalisation

The Criminal Law Revision Committee (CLRC) suggested that the time was coming when it might be advisable to also prosecute men who use the services of prostitutes and 'curb crawl' (CLRC 1984 p6). The increased visibility of such activities led to a change in view. However, Roger Matthews suggested that the Government was caught between wishing to introduce more controls and reducing the demands on the time of the courts and the police. So other alternatives were sought (1986 p193).

Should prostitution be legalised?

In response to the calls for legalisation mentioned in the introduction to this chapter a number of observers have noted that in Britain prostitution is not illegal but many of the surrounding activities are. Some academics have considered the possibility of making it illegal but rejected it as leading to decoy methods, entrapment or even questionable surveillance (Matthews 1986 p203). For example in the US the police officers have been known to follow couples into a motel room and then to open the door with a pass key or even knock it down. The couple are separated and interviewed and as the police could not expect the couple to admit guilt they would try to work out who solicited the immediate action and then use the evidence of the other to attempt to gain a conviction. This is obviously a difficult thing to attempt. In the Glasgow study of prostitutes forty five out of the fifty one (88%) believed that it should be legalised. Three opposed legalisation and one of these felt that it would encourage more young girls on to the streets and so introduce them to a dangerous way of life (Carr, Goldberg and Green 1994 p538).

There are a number of other arguments for legalisation. One is that it would be a benefit to the family in that if the men use prostitutes there would not be the threat to marriage as if they had affairs. Also prostitutes might be seen as providing a social service in that they were looking after the sexual needs of a group of men who could not maintain normal relationships or had peculiar sexual fantasies which might make their normal partner uncomfortable or themselves uncomfortable to reveal to their 'normal' woman. There is also an argument which I found common amongst building workers. This was that if there were a reliable and safe outlet for male sexuality it would reduce the number of rapes. There is also the argument that legalisation would enable regular health checks and so diminish the chance that venereal disease and AIDS would be spread. Furthermore, if the prostitute were under the protection of the state then she would not be so vulnerable from attacks from clients or pimps and it would also have the benefit to society in reducing the costs of the police and the courts and also would bring in income tax.

The disadvantages of legalisation are first that if society accepted prostitution it could be institutionalising a very conservative view of sexuality. Men would be seen as the seekers of sex and women the providers. A second problem is that a dual system is formed because only a percentage of prostitutes will register. This will then probably involve the state in being tougher with women still working the streets. Matthews argues:

Rather than 'solve' or reduce the problem of prostitution, it only encourages a contradictory system which on the one hand both encourages prostitution and its exploitation, while on the other hand it attempts to suppress prostitution and the prostitute (1986 p195).

However, there are good grounds for arguing a case for an approach which recognises the importance of sexuality and relationships to all.

Decriminalisation

The supporters of decriminalisation accept the inevitability of prostitution and also its role in support for the family and value to those using the women's service. It has attracted the support of a number of people and Matthews suggests several ideas have been put forward:

1 The first is that criminalisation of prostitution does not improve the situation but rather makes it worse.

2 Decriminalisation would reduce the social stigmatisation of the prostitute and allow her to work more openly.

3 Prostitution is a victimless crime and for this reason is not a suitable place for the intervention of the law.

4 In some senses the most important argument is that the average prostitute comes from a socially deprived group and has been forced into prostitution to possibly support her family or a drug habit which has developed out of poverty and the need to escape. If she should suffer again for being a prostitute she would be a double victim of society (Matthews 1986 p196)

5 It would overcome difficulties with the law by removing the problem. One of the of the difficulties is that once a woman has been labelled as a 'common prostitute' she can easily be persecuted by the police with little protection.

6 It could help take women out of the control of pimps and other shady characters who might not treat her properly and may exploit her.

7 It would save time for the courts and the police in interventions which are ineffective or even counterproductive.

8 The laws are sexist. As they normally penalise the prostitute while allowing the man to be free it seems to support the idea that male sexuality should be allowed to run free. It also bolsters 'the structures of male dominance, male privilege and monogamy'.

9 The prosecution of a woman a 'common prostitute' gives too much discretion to the police who may therefore be open to corruption.

There are a number of arguments against decriminalisation. Elizabeth Wilson said that 'Wholesale decriminalisation would simply mean a free for all for men (Wilson 11983 p224). There could also be a great deal of disturbance for people in local neighbourhoods.

Roger Matthews in 1986 proposed a third alternative to legalisation and decriminalisation. As he opposed proscription he proposed regulation as an alternative. This he suggested would lead to *'an alternative type of radical regulationism which could channel socialist objectives'*. He continued to outline four general aims of policy. These are a commitment to general deterrence, the reduction of harassment with diminished annoyance and disturbance, the protection from coercion and exploitation and finally the reduction of commercialisation (1986 p205).

Chapter 11

Terrorist, Guerilla or Freedom Fighter

Violent Acts against the state impinge upon all of our lives. To the traveller it is of great concern that a number of planes have been blown up in mid air.

* On 23 June 1985 a bomb blew up an Air India Boeing 747 off the coast of Ireland with the loss of 329 lives.

* On 21 December 1988 a bomb blew up a Pan Am at Lockerbie in Scotland with a loss of 270 lives.

* On 18 July 1996 a TWA flight, just taken off from Kennedy Airport, came down off the coast of Long Island with a loss of 230 lives. Some evidence of a bomb has been found.

The threats to aircraft have meant a great increase in airport expenditure and fear amongst passengers as well as a tremendous loss of life. In addition there have been many acts of violence against buildings or people. In Britain the IRA has carried out numerous bombings against the state and various other countries have had to face up to violence. There has been something of a void in the explanation of such actions. For example in his book **Political Terrorism** Wardlaw comments blandly:

'We simply do not have sufficient empirical evidence of what makes an individual become a terrorist'(1989 pxiv).

This failure is problematical because it leads Government's to try to treat political actions as if they were criminal ones and to undertake policies which depend to a large degree on deterrence and punishment. These are notably ineffective against those like the ten Irish hunger strikers who starved themselves to death or against the Tamil Tiger who reportedly killed herself in order to assassinate Rajiv Ghandi.

The Governments and mass media of countries are very hostile to the violent incidents. However, one person's 'terrorist' is another's 'freedom fighter' and several previous terrorists have become leaders of their country. The first President of the Republic of Ireland was Eamon De Valera who was nearly executed for his part in the Easter uprising of 1916. Other examples are Menachim Begin who became Prime Minister of Israel and Nelson Mandella who became president of South Africa.

The central point of this chapter is that an analysis of contracultures will help us understand the underlying causes of violent acts.

Culture, subculture and contraculture

The importance of contracultures was first proposed by Yinger (1960) in a pathfinding article. Criminologists such as Cohen (1955) had been working on the role of subcultures as a cause of crime but Yinger suggested the term subculture was too loosely defined as 'culture within a culture'. He said it applied both to groups within the society and not necessarily in conflict with it, for example, regional, class or age groups, however, it was also used for sections of the society which had areas of conflict with the dominant culture. Consequently for some groups in conflict with the society Yinger proposed the term 'contraculture'. These he suggested would occur *whenever the normative system of a group contains as a primary element, a theme of conflict with the values of the dominant society.'* He distinguished subcultures from contraculture in several ways and said that while the values of most subcultures probably differ from the dominant society in some degree, with contracultures the conflict element is central and many of the values are specifically contradictory to the dominant society.

As an example Yinger proposed that the term contraculture could be applied to the jazz musicians described by Becker (1951).

Matza and Sykes (1961) criticised Yinger's theory as applied to youth and argued that delinquent contracultures do not exist because the young are not sufficiently isolated. David Downes, while generally sympathetic to Yinger's perspective, argues that *'the validity of employing the concept of contraculture has yet to be proved - its adoption at this stage would serve to pre-judge the issue which Yinger has been at pains to clarify' (1966 p11).'*

The first clear evidence of the existence of (secular) contracultures came from the unpublished PhD of Jock Young (1968) and his findings amongst students. He found the existence of two polar kinds of contracultures. First the Marxists who wanted to overthrow the society by large scale changes in the social structure and secondly the hippies who wanted to change the world by a process of changing individuals. Their view was that eventually by a process of osmosis the bureaucratic networks would change. One of his important findings was that a key to the whole issue was their interpretation of the world. He said that the bohemian young smoked marijuana, not only because it was physically suitable and accessible in areas in which they live, but also because it was a symbol of identification with the values of a new order and had a moral component. Contracultural groups oppose the society and have a vision as to the method of change. Some believe that violence will be the catalyst. For example when Charles Manson's group killed Sharon Tate and her companions it believed it was helping to start the war to end all wars-**Helter Skelter** (Burgloisi 1977). Similarly, when the IRA is taking action it believes it is working towards the establishment of a free socialist Ireland (Beresford 1987 p64). So it is often the philosophy and world view which holds the key to understanding such actions.

By the time I first began reading what the criminologists had to say about contracultures I had a great deal of primary information on the Marxist and Hippie contracultures of the 1960s based on participant observation. I then began research into other historical and contemporary groups both to discover further characteristics of contracultures and also to analyse the conditions under which they are likely to arise. From this information I have analysed a number of important characteristics.

There have been a number of books which have drawn attention to similarities between political groups and religious contracultures. For example Robert Tucker stated:

'Marxism invites analysis as a religious system. It follows in certain ways the pattern of the great religious conceptions in Western culture. In particular, it has a number of basic characteristics in common with the Christian system in its Augustinian and later medieval expression (1965 p22).'

The similarities to which he drew attention were that both told a story that had a beginning, middle and an end with paradise being lost and regained. Both Augustine and Marx saw the latest period as being the time of *'deepest suffering, and the prelude to the final revolution* (1965 p23). Tucker also drew comparison between the idea of salvation of the individual in Christianity and the spiritual regeneration of people in Marxism.

Tucker intended his analysis as being a way to debunk Marx. The approach of our analysis is to say that there are bound to be similarities between certain religious groups and Marxism because they are both contracultures. However, they need to be distinguished because societal contracultures like Marxism believe that social change must come about by the actions of people rather than by the deity.

Characteristics of contracultures

a) **They develop from deviant subcultures** These fall into four main subgroups (Cohen 1955).

i) <u>Ascribed</u> This applies to homosexual subcultures. The individuals do not have a choice about the nature of their deviance. They can only make decisions about whether to 'come out' and challenge society by saying they are, for example, 'glad to be gay', or instead try and merge into society.

ii) <u>Obtained</u> In this case the individuals choose to disobey society in order to fight for the greater social good such as the white liberals who fought apartheid in South Africa.

iii) <u>Socially determined</u> The position of certain groups in terms of the dominant subculture leads to the individuals being socialised into deviance. This is the case with the Catholics in Northern Ireland or the Palestinians.

iiii) <u>Transitional</u> The youth subcultures of some teenagers become deviant for a short period in response to the conflicts of school, work or the family. These individuals will then often merge with the dominant culture and become more conformist as their personal situation alters.

Sometimes changes in the social situation will lead to deviant subcultures becoming increasingly alienated from the dominant culture so that they become contracultures. When this happens the deviant groups will go beyond aiming for specific social changes and want total change in society. A good example of this was in the USA in 1960s. The Students for a Democratic Society (SDS) at first deviated only slightly from the dominant culture. The President Lyndon Johnson was campaigning with a slogan 'All the Way with LBJ'. The SDS campaigned with 'part of the way with LBJ' showing that they thought he was the best of the available alternatives. However, as the war in Vietnam continued a group broke away from the SDS and formed the Weathermen. This group sided with the Vietnamese cause and declared war on the United States (Lauter and Howe 1970 p22). From 1st January 1969 to

15th April 1970 they killed forty people and injured 384 in over 4,000 reported bombings (Francome 1976 p232).

In Ireland it was the failure of the civil rights movement which produced the conditions under which violent contracultural groups developed in the 1968s. Contracultures may exist in a very small way for many years until the social conditions change to a position where they have wider appeal. An example of this is bohemian groups of the 1950s which were small until the war in Vietnam and the growth of the youth movement in the 1960s. So the development of contracultures from deviant subcultures is one characteristic.

b) **The three kinds of contracultures**. They can be classified according to their belief in the means of change of the society.

i) Individualist contracultures These locate the problems within the individual. They want to change society by means of osmosis whereby people spread ideas on a personal level. Very often these groups will assert that there are no actions which are inherently evil but it is simply that society makes the rules for people to follow. We have seen that Becker said that their rules are promoted by moral entrepreneurs. To members of individualistic contracultures the infringement of arbitrary rules is a sensible protest against society and by people breaking the straight jacket they will gradually liberate themselves. Others will follow their example and eventually the whole society will be changed. These groups do not see the necessity of organised political action but concentrate on living a life that they see as embodying the perfect values. This is the approach of groups such as the early Quakers and Ranters and later the Bohemians and Hippies (Hill 1975 pp184-258, Leary 1968 pp224-36). Timothy Leary's exhortation to young people to *'turn on, tune in, drop out'* is a good example of the individualistic approach.

ii) <u>Societal contracultures</u> These take the view that it is society that is inherently evil. Once the social structure has been changed the situation will have developed for good personal development. This was the position taken by the Diggers at the time of the English Revolution and is also the contemporary Marxist position. The belief is that once the revolution has occurred then a totally different kind of society will develop. People will be able to be different because the society in which they were born and raised has changed.

iii) <u>Religious contracultures</u> These are often known as sects. They regard the world as fundamentally 'evil and full of sin'. However, they look to divine intervention in order to produce social change. So the Jehovah's Witnesses expect that God will soon bring about the end of the world, raise up the dead members of the sect and form a paradise on earth. Other examples of religious contracultures are the early Christians, the Hussites and the first Mormons.

Usually in practice these theoretical distinctions will be blurred and contracultures will have both social and religious aspects. For example Charles Manson believed that the carrying out of violent acts would spark a war- 'helter skelter'- which would eventually lead to him ruling the world. However, he also used the book of Revelations as part of his explanation. So there was a strong mystical side in his theory (Bugloisi and Gentry 1977).

c) **Contracultures tend to contain a high number of young people** There are a number of reasons for this.

* Young people have much less stake in the established order.

* The young have fewer material possessions and will benefit from any redistribution of wealth.

* They are also freer of family responsibilities.

* Youth is a period of transition. With increasing age young people liberate themselves from the restrictions of childhood and so change is likely to be seen in a positive light.

* Young people are also more likely to find complete explanations of the world appealing, especially as they may not have been exposed to certain ideas such as Marxism or Militant Christianity before.

* Students are generally relatively isolated from the dominant culture. The media on the campus may well be quite different from that in the rest of the society.

Historically, periods when for demographic reasons there were great increases in the number of young people were also those where contracultural developments were most likely. The Protestant reformation in Europe has been called one of the outstanding youth movements in history and it was linked to an increase in the number of students (Williams 1962) Similarly in the period 1960-70 the number of those aged 14-24 increased by 52% in the United States. This combined by the growth in student numbers and the war in Vietnam led to it being a period where various contracultural groups developed.

d) **There is a tendency towards polarisation** This is especially the case in terms of attitudes to violence, sexuality and drugs. Many contracultures such as the Jehovah's Witnesses are totally opposed to violence, whilst Charles Manson's group regarded it as a necessary development in order to create the new society. Other groups such as the Weathermen also regarded violence as a way to achieve their aims.

Some religious sects were opposed to sexuality. The Shakers banned it totally and except for David Koresh, the leader, male members of the Wako group were banned from intercourse. In contrast other contracultures took a very liberal view. The

190

Mormons in the early days practised polygamy, some of the hippies had the slogan 'Make love not war', and the Dukobours use to parade around naked to protest against the values of the wider society.

Most Christian contracultures will oppose drugs which they see as a temptation. The Mormons are opposed even to caffeine in coffee. The Marxists generally are not opposed to alcohol but see other drugs as a diversion from the main activity. Some of the individualist contracultures regard drugs as the key to changing people and predicted that one day the President of the USA would take them. They were right in that Clinton admitted to smoking marijuana, although he claimed he did not inhale.

e) **Contracultures are in a dynamic relationship with the dominant society, the deviant subcultures and other contracultures.** In times of stress there will usually be several different contracultural groups formed with different beliefs and at different levels of social distance from the dominant culture. These will try and obtain converts from each other and there will be a debate on the correctness of each position. One central issue is whether to work for small changes to improve conditions or rather to accept the argument that working for small changes will be counterproductive because it will ameliorate the situation and delay the much more fundamental change they deem necessary.

Members of societal contracultures will try and persuade those of individualistic ones that they will not change society by individual activities. So the Marxists in the 1960s used to argue with hippies that the capitalists are not going to be worried by a few people sitting round and smoking pot. In 1967 Peace News printed a front page article entitled 'The case against the drug culture' in which a Berkeley activist argued that the whole LSD/marihuana debate was simply escapism *'the latest opium of the people in a more literal and potentially more dangerous sense than anything envisaged by Karl Marx'* (Anderson).

In contrast the hippies criticised Marxists for not wanting to change themselves and for not having a good time. One incident that occurred during the height of the strike at the LSE in 1967 was that a group of hippies interrupted a heavy debate by marching through the lecture theatre jingling bells and proclaiming their message of love. Timothy Leary criticised the Berkeley student protesters in the following terms: *'Berkeley activists and rebels haven't dropped out. Rather, they act as dupes within the system'.* In answer to an interviewer in 1966 he claimed it was not important to change the system but rather the individual (Francome 1976 p241). The interviewer said that many former campus activists who had taken LSD were more concerned with what was happening in their own heads rather than the world at large. Leary replied: *'The insight of LSD leads you to concern yourself more with the internal or spiritual values; you realise that it doesn't make any difference what you do on the outside unless you change the inside* (Francome 1976 p242).

f) **There is an inverse relationship between the nearness of the expected rapid change in the social order and the degree of co-operation with the dominant culture.** This is in part because groups who expect the change to be soon do not want to waste time building channels of communication which might be time consuming. If (as usual) the expected change does not occur there may be some dissatisfaction within the group and pressure to co-operate with others who are of a similar persuasion. When this happens the leadership may stick to its original position and expel those who deviate from the official line. This is what happened with the British Workers Revolutionary Party in 1975. However, the leadership may decide to take a more liberal approach to co-operation. This will entail limiting objectives and implies that the larger change will occur after some minor objectives have been achieved.

g) **Contracultural groups are a dominant part of the person's life.** At the LSE in 1965/6 a Marxist contraculture evolved with a core of about twelve members. They joined the organisation which was to become the Socialist Workers Party and the group dominated their lives. They spent much of their time reading and debating and taking views on political issues. They were very opposed to the major political parties. If one member of the group was invited to a party then the whole group would be told and they would be likely to arrive together. When the group decided that there was not enough culture in society there was the unlikely sight of all the group dancing around the gym at the LSE. For the member's the group's approval was crucial and they spent a very large part of their social life in activities related to it.

Other contracultural groups also called for great commitment even to the extent of individuals giving their lives for the cause as we have seen.

h) **Contracultures tend to oppose the nuclear family** There will be a number of situations in which family responsibilities will come in between the perceived needs of the group. Earlier the Marxists criticism of the family were discussed. Andrew Rigby, in discussing the commune movement in Britain, quoted from one of its pamphlets:

The monogamous family in its traditional isolation is the greatest barrier to all social reform as well an ultimately, the instrument of the most devastating form of grief known and we urge its abolition (Rigby 1974 p316).

i) **Contracultural Groups are prone to split**. Groups which are further in social distance from the dominant society are more likely to do so. These schisms may occur because of differences over doctrine which may appear to outsiders to be relatively obscure. They may also result from other factors such as the degree of co-operation with the dominant culture or even other contracultures.

193

j) **Contracultures are led by a charismatic leader** The disciples follow the leader because of his or her personal qualities and the following is voluntary. If the leader dies then more bureaucratic methods of selecting a leader may be chosen.

k) **Contracultures have a belief system**

There will be a rationale for their actions and the way in which change will occur. Sometimes, especially amongst religious contracultures, it may not seem too sensible to members of the dominant culture. However, the groups usually have some sources of legitimate complaint which underlines their position.

l) **Disparate groups may cause a revolution**. Marx believed that a revolution would occur by a united working class in which all the members had the same interests. However, as discussed in chapter five, history has shown that when a revolution occurs it is by a variety of groups with different interests uniting against the dominant group. However, then there will need to be a power struggle to see which of the groups will take over and most groups will be disappointed. A good example of this was in Iran. Both the left wing and right wing groups joined forces in the revolution. However, after it was over the Ayatollahs fought and attacked many members of the left wing Mujaheden.

m) **Usual theories of punishment are not relevant** Members of contracultures will often be willing to die for their cause. They will therefore not be subject to the normal constraints or theories of criminal justice. The 'terrorists' will see themselves as freedom fighters and such threats as capital punishment will often not appear relevant to them. If fact numerous people have given up their lives.

* Ten IRA hunger strikers killed themselves.

* Two men drove their truck filled with explosives into the US army barracks in Beirut.

* A women killed herself in order to assassinate Rajiv Ghandi.

* Various suicide bombers have killed many people in Israel (occupied Palestine). The Guardian reported on 5th March 1996:

'Islamist fanatics dealt out mass murder for the fourth time in eight days with a suicide bomb which killed 12 civilians'. (Brown)

n) **There will be paradise after the revolution** One of the consistent features of contracultural groups is that after the great change there will be a period during which everyone is happy. The Jehovah's Witnesses believe the dead will be raised up and there will be peace which will last a thousand years. The hippies believed that one day everyone would be happy because they would be smoking pot. The Marxists look to a period of communism when there will be no alienation and no property crime.

o) **Increased media attention** Margaret Mead argued that those born in the post 1944 period were brought up in an age where television and the other media has made the world a smaller place. The young were brought up in a different world from their parents so she said those born pre 1944 were 'immigrants in time' (Mead 1970).

There is no doubt that with the age of television acts of violence are given much more prominent publicity. This may give groups an exaggerated view of their own importance.

p) **The revolutionary change may not occur** Or if the revolution does happen it may well be 'betrayed' in the eyes of many of the contracultures by the group taking over. If the dominant culture is inflexible and does not listen to the grievances of the contracultural groups and the deviant subcultures from which they sprang then the discontent will continue.

q) **Exporting violent action** A change in the position from previous centuries is that some states will support guerrilla activity in other countries. Furthermore the sharing of information has led to widespread availability of the means to carry out violent actions. One of the allegations is against Iran. In the aftermath of several suicide bombings the Israeli ambassador to the United Nations was quoted as saying:

'Iran is one of the main supporters, instigators, supplying training facilities, arms and political support for these groups' (Walker 1996).

There were also allegations that Libya supported guerrilla groups in other countries.

So these are the major features of contracultural groups. The headings will form the basis as we now consider two examples of contracultural groups which have committed violence:

Examples of contracultural groups

Charles Manson and murders committed by his group

On 9th August 1969 Sharon Tate, the wife of Roman Polanski, the film director and seven months pregnant, was murdered in Los Angeles together with four other people. She was found with a rope around her neck, as was Jay Sebring her former hairdresser boyfriend. There were messages from the killers. The word 'pig' was written on the front door in her blood. On the wall of the living room were written the words 'POLITICAL PIGGY' in another victims blood (Bugliosi 1977 ed p46).

The following day (10 August 1969) two more bodies Leno and Rosemary Bianca were found stabbed to death. Leno had an ivory handled carving fork protruding from his stomach. There was writing in three places in the residence. High up on the living room wall was printed DEATH TO PIGS. On another wall was the single word RISE and on the refrigerator door was written two words-the first misspelled-HEALTER SKELTER (Cavendish 1992 p43).

The murders led to panic. In two days one Beverley Hills sporting goods store sold 200 firearms, when before the slayings they had sold three or four a day. In order to understand the background to the killings let us consider the major characteristics of Manson's contraculture:

It developed from deviant subcultures

The student culture in the 1960s was very opposed to the dominant culture. There was growing alienation as young people increasingly disbelieved the justification for the War in Vietnam. A piece of research showed developing cynicism towards the major social institutions (Hockreich and Rotter 1970). A member of Berkeley Student Strike Committee commented on what they saw as the vacuous nature of USA society.

The war in Vietnam shows many students that American Foreign policy is all too frequently brutal and coercive...many whites are unable to deal with their own racism.... A large and growing number of university students are unwilling to live out their lives in the emptiness of middle class America. And in the midst of all this, most books coming out of academia argue that America's major problems have been solved and all we have to do now is to tie up he loose ends. But students feel that America's problems have not been solved and they are searching for ways of understanding these problems and taking action that will solve them (Francome 1976 p224).

Overall there were a wide range of student protest activities ranging from those which were within the system such as support for radical anti-war politicians to the draft burning groups. The war widened the cultural gap between the student subcultures and the dominant ideology (Francome 1976 p222-226).

At the time there were also a wide variety of hippie groups. John Lennon had said in the song revolution *'You better change your mind instead'*. Many of them were into peace and love. Manson saw pacifism as weakness and like the Weathermen polarised towards violence. In fact there is evidence that Manson's murders were welcomed by other contracultures. Bernadine Dorn told an SDS convention:

'Offing those rich pigs with their own forks and knives, and then eating a meal in the same room, far out. The Weathermen dig Charles Manson (Bugliosi 1977 ed p270).

The underground newspaper *Tuesday's Child* which claimed to be the voice of the Yippies put Manson's picture on the front page naming him MAN OF THE YEAR.

It has a strong belief system

Manson taught his members who accepted his view of the world.

One of the group members Susan Atkins believed Charles Manson when he told her that there was a hole in Death Valley and he was the only person who knew where it was. Deep down in the middle of the earth there was a civilisation in a bottomless pit and the chosen few were to be taken there. One of the stories his members believed was that Manson found a dead bird, breathed on it and it flew away (Bugliosi 1977 ed p235).

Manson often quoted from Revelation chapter nine in support of his own views. He was also obsessed with the Beatles and found a multitude of meanings in their songs. The white album was particularly significant to the Family and in the song Blackbird there is a line.

'You were only waiting for this moment to arise. (Bugliosi 1977 ed p297)'

This was interpreted as a call for the black man to rise up and take his turn. George Harrison's song 'piggies' talked of middle classes getting a damned good whacking. Bugliosi commented:

'I couldn't listen to the final stanza without visualising what happened at 3301 Waverly Drive. It describes piggy couples dining out, in all their starched finery, eating bacon with forks and knives. Rosemary La Bianca: forty one knife wounds. Leno La Bianca, twelve knife wounds, punctured with a fork seven times, a knife in his throat, a fork in his stomach and, on the wall, in his own blood, DEATH TO PIGS'(1977 p298).

Such violence was carried out by Manson's family members is initially surprising and difficult to comprehend. It seems it was possible because the Family members were well indoctrinated to follow his instructions. They were also such strong believers of Manson's views-to such a degree that Bugliosi said of them:

'They seemed to radiate inner contentment. I'd seen others like this-true believers, religious fanatics...There was no need to search any more they had found the truth. And their truth was 'Charlie is love'.... On asking where they were on a certain date, they'd reply "There is no such thing as time" (Bugliosi 1977 ed p161).'

There is a tendency towards polarisation Manson's 'Family' was both sexist and racist. In Manson's family there were five females to every male (Bugliosi 1977 ed p274). The women were taught that their purpose in life was to look after men and have babies.

The group polarised towards violence which they saw as the way that 'Helter Skelter' would be started and the new world brought about.

Apart from the murders mentioned above there were others. At one the murderer made a paw print in blood on the wall with the aim 'to push the blame on the black panthers (Bugliosi 1977 ed p125). These used the paw print as a symbol.

In a Beatles album the song Revolution says 'you can count me out' but immediately afterwards says 'in'. This was interpreted by Manson to mean that the Beatles favoured the revolution. What Manson was probably not aware about was that John Lennon was at the time moving towards Marxism rather than Manson's interpretation (Francome 1976).

Manson believed that the black groups of the world would rise up and take over the country. The purpose of the murders were to start the race war 'Helter Skelter'. This was to be the final war on the planet the 'war to end all wars'. It would result in the black men emerging triumphant and they would kill all the white men except those hiding in the desert.

There were a high number of young people

Coleman pointed out that the baby boom starting in 1946 caused a great increase in young people. During the decade 1960-70 there was a 52% increase in young people aged 14-24. This meant there were many more people with potential for deviance. and a few of them were attracted to Manson's position.

The extent of contracultural deviation from the dominant society is a process of interaction. The Manson group was pleased when their women had their children within the group. This was a sign of the groups separation from the society. However, the group needed money for some activities and so had to accept the dominant culture to a degree.

The fact that Manson could provide young women willing to have sex made him attractive to various men. It could be that others were attracted to drugs. So there was a constant flow of people to and from the commune.

Contracultures are led by a charismatic leader

Manson was born in 1934 and he was not closely cared for by his parents. He was often in prison but while inside he had learned that things had changed outside and the conservative world had been replaced. He left prison on 21 March 1967 and commented on the new situation:

'Pretty girls were running around every place with no panties or bras and asking for love. Grass and hallucinatory drugs were being handed out to you in the streets. It was a different world than I had ever been in and one that I believed was too good to be true. It was a convict's dream and after being locked up for seven solid years, I didn't run from it. I joined it and the generation that lived in it. (Cavendish 1992 p47).

By July 1969 Manson was leader of a primitive commune of around 30-35 people. He had a totally different background from those who followed him.

There will be paradise after the revolution Charlie would lead his family into the desert where they would multiply until they became 144,000. This figure is the same as that mentioned by the Jehovah's Witnesses and probably comes from Revelation Chapter Seven which mentions twelve tribes of Israel each numbering 12,000 (Bugliosi 1977 ed p284). The family would then emerge from the bottomless pit and there would only be the family and black servants and Charlie Manson would rule the world (Bugliosi 1977 ed p304).

The revolutionary change may not occur In Manson's case the revolution was never going to occur. There was a problem that the black people were not rising up and so Manson believed that he had to show the way (Bugliosi 1977 ed p305). On Friday 8th August 1969 Manson told the family *'Now is the time for Helter Skelter'*.
Susan Atkins, one of Manson's group was arrested on another count and while in prison told her former call-girl cell mate that she carried out the Sharon Tate murder because:

We wanted to do a crime that would shock the world, that the world would have to stand up and take notice.. I felt so elated tired, but at peace with myself. I knew that this was the beginning of Helter Skelter. (Bugliosi 1977 ed p99)

In a trial that lasted nine months Manson was convicted on nine counts of murder.

The Irish Republican Army This is a much different kind of contractultural group from that of Manson with a clear aim of a United Ireland. It is, however, the group with the greatest amount of violence against the state in Britain. The IRA is a mature organisation which in many respects is a different kind of organisation from the contracultures. However, it still has strong contracultural aspects which it is useful to identify. Let us consider the movement within the general headings for characteristics of contracultures.

They develop from deviant subcultures. The Irish revolt against English rule began in 1641 and eight years of warfare followed. The British believed that the Irish were rebels who in opposing their rule sinned against divine law. One order to the British generals 28th February 1642 commanded *'burn, spoil, waste, consume and demolish all places, towns and houses where the said rebels are or have been relieved and harboured, and all hay and corn there, and kill and destroy all the men inhabiting, able to bear arms (Macardle 1937 p33).*

Oliver Cromwell wrote after his troops massacred almost the whole population of Drogheda including women and children. *'It has pleased God to bless our endeavours'(Macardle 1937 p33).* The British subjected the Irish by using the legal system to punish Catholics. There were calls for a 'free and independent Republic of Ireland' in 1803 (Macardle 1937 p45).

The subjection of the Irish led to the great famine of the nineteenth century. It had become more profitable to export cattle to England than to grow crops (Macardle 1937 p42). The Times reported in 1845 that the Island was full and overflowing with food but that it was not getting to the *'hungry mouths'*. The Landlords were getting their money but *'hundreds of poor people had lain down and died on the roadsides'* (Macardle 1937 p42). Lord John Russell commented in the House of Lords (23 March 1846):

'We have made it (Ireland) the most degraded and most miserable country in the world.'

The Irish population fell from 8.3 million in 1843 to 6.2 million in 1851 and 4.4 million by 1911 (Macardle 1937 p42-4).

The partitioning of Ireland in 1921 led to the Catholics in the North being in a minority. There they faced discrimination which is one factor leading to them having a different perspective from the Protestants. Although only a minority Catholics in the north may support the violence of the IRA they will have sympathy for some of its aims. The fact that Bobbie Sands could be elected an MP while in prison shows the fact that the IRA does have a degree of grass roots support.

It has a strong belief system

The Irish Socialist Workers Party was founded by James Connelly in 1896 and two years later he started and edited *The Worker's Republic*. The aim was to join together the cause of Irish labour with independence. He wrote:

The Irish working class must emancipate itself and in emancipating itself, it must perforce, free its country.... Only the Irish working class remain as the incorruptible inheritors of the fight for freedom in Ireland (Macardle 1937 p58).

We can see strong Marxist overtones in such analysis. Another factor which is important is the memory of the 1916 Easter uprising. Part of the Proclamation of the Irish Republic issued on Easter Monday 1916 said:

The Republic guarantees religious and civil liberty, equal rights and equal opportunities to all its citizens, and declares its resolve to pursue the happiness and prosperity of the whole nation and of all its parts (Macardle 1937 p157).

The proclamation also made clear that the men were willing to die for their cause and Patrick Pearse the martyred leader wrote a poem for his mother in which he identified himself with Christ (O'Toole 1996).

One of the leaders of the revolt was Eamon de Valera. He escaped execution and eventually was elected head of the Republic. The decision on Irish independence led to the six counties in the North being divided from the rest of the country to become part of the United Kingdom. They have a protestant majority.

Young Irish Catholics are socialised into the republican cause. Sean O'Callaghan, a former IRA activist, who assassinated two people stated:

'Like the great mass of Irish people I was educated in my early years at school by nuns and Christian Brothers. The Brothers had a fierce nationalist ethos. They saw themselves as the moral guardians of nationalist Ireland. It was world of Gaelic games, the Irish language, and endless songs and stories about noble Irish patriots and treacherous English. The treachery of the English was the root of all Ireland's ills (1996).

<u>There is a tendency towards polarisation</u> This is especially the case in terms of attitudes to violence. IRA also in some conditions regard violence as a way to achieve its aims. Violence is not usually done while angry but in the belief that it will lead to desirable ends. O'Callaghan commented: *'It would be utterly wrong to see these young men universally as lurid , evil psychopaths. That they carried out the most awful acts of violence is beyond question. But the real blame lies with their leadership, the old republican/ nationalists who instilled discipline, obedience and a reverence for republican structures and traditions that allowed young men to kill even former friends for minor transgressions of the republican code'.*

O'Callaghan is now opposed to the IRA and those more sympathetic might challenge the final allegation.

<u>The extent of contracultural deviation from the dominant society is a process of interaction.</u> The IRA is well aware of the norms of the dominant society the effects of different kinds of action and direct its actions accordingly. In most cases especially with guerilla groups the path of deviance is deliberately chosen with the group rejecting the interpretation the dominant culture places on their behaviour. They see themselves as freedom fighters.

<u>Contracultural groups are a dominant part of the person's life.</u>

It is mainly young men and women (less often) who are recruited into the IRA. It provides them with a purpose in life and status in the community and they are working for a cause in which they believe.

O'Callaghan said *'These were young men without much hope of employment who had seen their communities devastated in sectarian attacks. Now they were hitting back their pride and dignity was restored (1996).'*

<u>Contracultural Groups are prone to split</u>. So the Provisionals split off from the IRA to take a more militant line. There were other splits too.

<u>Contracultures are led by a charismatic leader</u> The leadership of groups like the IRA are kept secret for security purpose. The highly visible officers of Sein Feine such as Gerry Adams do not appear to have too much power. For example it seems unlikely that Adams supported the return of hostilities in 1996 but was powerless to stop it (Sharrock 1996).

<u>Disparate groups may cause a revolution</u>. We have seen Marx believed that a revolution would occur by a united working class in which all the members had the same interests. However if a revolution were to occur in Ireland it would be likely to be against the wishes of the Protestant working class.

<u>Usual theories of punishment are not relevant</u>

The ten IRA hunger strikers killed themselves for their cause. This is a very difficult and painful way to die and the martyrs went blind before dying. Bobby Sands when facing death drew comfort from the image of James Connolly the rebel's military commander and wrote in his diary (O'Toole 1996):

'I always keep thinking of James Connolly, and the great calm and dignity that he showed right to his very end, his courage and resolve... I may die, but the Republic of 1916 will never die.'

When people are willing to go to such lengths it is clear that the depth of their belief is such that they are not going to be dissuaded from fear of Government action.

There will be paradise after the revolution The members of the IRA look forward to the day when there is a 32 county republic. This would be a socialist country which could only come about by force.

Increased media attention The IRA is well aware of the publicity of different acts. They knew that bombings in Britain would have more effect publicity wise than those in Ireland and took this into account with their actions.

The revolutionary change may not occur

After thirty years of troubles it does not seem that a united Ireland is likely. The guerillas will then have to decide what is the best action to take. As religion is such a divisive factor the setting up of a secular state might be the most likely way a united Ireland could occur. However, there are few signs of this happening. The setting up of the European Union may also make the nationalist calls seem somewhat less potent if people begin to transcend local boundaries and begin thinking in terms of International ones.

Exporting violent action The IRA have received a great amount of money from the USA and the links go back a long time. In 1858 the Irish Republican Brotherhood was founded in the USA (Macardle 1937 p45). People of the USA often state that Ireland is Britain's Vietnam and have helped finance guerilla action.

Discussion I suggest that looking at contracultural theory is a useful way considering terrorist actions. By a realisation that they arise from deviant subcultures and the fact that traditional punishments have very limited validity it can help keep Governments from naive actions. When the two men drove their lorry load of explosives into the American base in Lebanon killing themselves and over two hundred and fifty soldiers President Reagan called them 'cowards'. This they were clearly not. However misguided others think they may have been the suicide bombers are not cowards. It must have taken great will power and a strong belief in their cause to take such action.

The long term solution to terrorism cannot be simply be the right wing one of catching and punishing the perpetrators. In fact such action may lead to even greater dissent and more people joining the contracultural group. A suicide bomb killed 25 people in Israel exactly two years after the Hebron massacre when Baruch Goldstein killed 29 Palestinians in a mosque. In response Palestinian police rounded up forty Hamas activists. The report in the <u>Guardian</u> said more arrests were likely (Brown and Berry 1996). This kind of action could well be counter productive. It could lead to greater dissent from these people who may be innocent of any crime. It is also likely to increase the alienation of the community and lead to more social stress. The only real way to get rid of 'terrorism' is to eliminate the injustices which cause it.

Chapter 12

The Crime Solution

I made it clear in the introduction that it would be impossible to totally get rid of crime. However, there is no doubt that its incidence was very much lower in earlier times and could be made much lower now. Evidence from different countries and regions also show wide variations which indicates that changed socialisation in the countries and areas with high rates could lead to a reduction in criminality.

We have discussed the attitude of the right wing and the view that a return to the traditional family is a solution to crime. However, even if it were possible to return to nineteenth century family patterns it is by no means clear that this would be a solution. Crime rates were very high in the last century and there were high rates of violence, murder, theft, prostitution and illegal abortion. Furthermore we have noted that there is no clear evidence that the 'broken home' causes an increase in crime.

In chapter Four the New York repression of crime was discussed. The question is whether such an approach would be of value to the British police force. There are some doubts because, for example, when in 1995 the Metropolitan Police launched operation 'Eagle Eye', an anti mugging campaign it had limited success. Despite the fact that arrests increased by 76 per cent the rates of street robberies increased (Campbell 1996). There is also the criticism that if police are repressing minor crimes they will not have the resources to deal with the major ones.

The evidence indicates that progress in reducing crime will more likely be made by improving overall socialisation. In order to achieve this a number of social changes need to be made.

1) **Reduce inequality** We have seen that there has been a movement towards an increased amount of poverty. In part this has been the steady result of policies designated to reduced the position of the poorer groups such as the abolition of maternity allowance. However, in many cases the inequality has been produced spectacularly. In the middle 1990s it seems that virtually every month there were stories in the newspapers of people becoming very wealthy because the Government sold off the national assets cheaply. For example, the Guardian reported:

'A former British Rail terminal manager, Sandy Anderson, was last night set to reap a bonus of £39.9 million made in only seven months from the sale of his train leasing company, in what was described by Labour as "the biggest privatisation scandal of them all" (Harper and Atkinson 1996 p1).'

When Ted Heath was Prime Minister he often talked about a 'fair days work for a fair days pay'. This kind of view which implies that people should make what contribution they can to society for reasonable is undermined by changes where people see the already rich netting millions of pounds.

A move towards a more equal society is likely to improve the crime rates and also we know that the overall health of society is better in countries where there is greater equality (Francome and Marks 1996).

2) **Support families** There is also a strong case for the government providing extra support. This has been whittled away over the years especially with the removal of maternity benefits and the reductions during the period when child support was frozen. It meant that increasing numbers of families were suffering financial hardship. It is time for the society to recognise parenting whether in single parent or two parent households as a very important activity. In this respect we might take up some of the proposals of Utting. These came under three headings

<u>Universal services</u> Each family should have the support of a range of services such as parent eduction programmes, course for improving parenting skills, good quality child care for those who wish to work, pre-school education and family planning and preparation for life classes in schools.

<u>Neighbourhood prevention</u> Any targeting of services should be on high crime neighbourhoods and not specific families. This could include community policing and preventive work with families, after school clubs and holiday activities for children, improved housing management of high crime estates and an increase in open access family centres offering a variety of services to families.

<u>Family preservation</u> For certain families, especially those which have come to the attention of the social services, there should be intensive care services delivered in their own homes.

A similar approach was proposed by Shepherd and Farrington who suggest:

The best way to prevent crime and violence seems to be by family support, training of parents, preschool education and modifying opportunities for crime (1995 p271).

Evidence of randomised experiments appear to show long term benefits by targeting single parents, poorly educated families with pre school children and those with low income. They suggest that four studies which showed long term falls in delinquency all addressed multiple risk factors (Shepherd and Farrington 1995 p271).

* The Perry Pre school project concentrated on African-American families with low incomes and children aged 3-5 (Berrueta-Clement, Schweinhart, Bamett et al 1984)

* The Houston study concentrated on Mexican-American families

with low incomes and children aged 1-3 (Johnson and Walker 1987).

* The Syracuse family project provided services to mothers with less than high school education and low incomes whose children were under the age of five (Lally, Mangione, Honig and Wittner 1988).

* The New York Project did not wait for birth but targeted pregnant women (Olds, Henderson, Chamberlain and Tatelbaum 1986).

All these projects entailed advice being provided by either home visitors-usually nurses- or by teachers at pre- school programmes. The home visitors provided mothers with parenting advice which included help with nutrition, child development and how to avoid substance abuse. It seems that the most successful programmes were those that combined educating parents and training children in social skills while they were in primary grades (Shepherd and Farrington 1995 p271).

Family lawyer Ruth Fine and myself have been carrying out research into contact between fathers and their children after separation/divorce. This is at the request of the National Council for One Parent Families and we found that one third of fathers no longer had contact with their children after separation. These could have had an important general role to play in their children' personality development which in certain circumstances could have prevented delinquency. We will be making some recommendations as how to improve the situation. However, Patricia Hewitt's suggestion that unmarried fathers should have equal rights to married ones is in the right direction. In a policy document for the Institute of Public Policy Research she called for society to encourage strong, loving and lasting bonds between fathers and their children (Boseley 1996).

Overall there is a strong case for giving families extra support in order that crime can be reduced.

3) **New Values** The policies which have been operating in Britain have been based on selfishness. We have seen that the philosophy behind the new right is that the greatest good for society is based upon people seeking their own interests. They should look after themselves and family. The right wing economics underlying government policy encourages the belief that it is better for people to seek their own ends. However, this philosophy neglects the value of altruism and people working together as teams.

In addition such developments as the national lottery have led to people that luck is the way ahead. For many it is the new opiate - the dream that will take them out of their present situation.

This kind of individualistic approach to values presents the pre-conditions that may lead to people breaking the law to support their own selfish ends. However, it is possible to have different values and the education system is important here. Young people could be considering what they can contribute towards the society rather what they can receive from it. Richard Titmuss outlined the importance of altruism in his book **The Gift Relationship**. He noted that in some societies people provide blood because they care for others and they receive nothing in return. He maintained this system was better than other societies which persuaded people to give blood by pursuing their selfish interests and which gave rewards of cash. He also showed that the amount of altruism can vary between societies which can be a challenge. For if we can create a greater degree of altruism so people wish to help each other instead of competing, where people are seeking more to contribute that to receive, then we will be producing the kind of people who will not be committing crime.

4) **Gender differences** When looking at the rates of rape. One of the arguments was that societies with very segregated sex roles and

also a high degree of violence have more cases of rape. There is a case for making sex much less of a case where man is the pursuer and woman the pursued. In as much as men are required by the society to be sexually assertive and take the lead in initiating relationships while women are expected to be relatively 'pure' then there are clearly going to be wide differences in perspective. We can see that in these circumstances that rape is just the polar end of the 'normal' patterns of relationship. So greater sex equality can be an important development.

5) **The Role of punishment** We have seen from the European figures that there is very little logic in the use of punishment. There were claims by the Home Secretary Mr Howard that 'prison works' and that increasing the numbers of prisoners will reduce the crime levels (Travis 1996). However, activist Paul Cavadino of the Penal Affairs Consortium, an umbrella group for 27 organisations argued that the increase in crime at the end of 1995 showed once again that prison does not in fact work. He challenged;

'If the Government want to cut crime it must put its money into a comprehensive crime prevention strategy rather than imprisoning more and more offenders' (Travis 1996).

We have also seen that punishment does not work with contracultural groups. So while protection of the public and punishment will clearly continue to have its role, there needs to be recognition of its limits. A basic fairness is also important rather than what has been happening-which is that political decisions have altered the size of prison populations.

6) **Weapon control** There were some reductions in availability of weapons with the introduction of the 1988 Firearms Act introduced after the Hungerford massacre. The change, however, did not stop the Dunblane massacre of young children in 1996. In the wake of the latest tragedy the Parliamentary Home Affairs Select Committee considered a ban on handguns. However, the six

Conservative members of the group outvoted the five others on the committee to oppose a ban. The gun lobby has asked all its members to contribute £25 towards the cost of opposing restrictions and the power of the gun lobby was discussed by the bereaved parents of Dunblane. Isabel MacBeath, whose five year old daughter was killed commented:

'*We are not as naive as some people like to think. We knew that they were people with money and clout and that they would try to swing opinion. We are just disappointed that they seem to have some success with the Tories on the Home Affairs Committee.* (Mills and Arlidge 1996).'

In Chapter two I gave examples of eighteen examples of mass murder which occurred in one incident and a total of 216 people were killed in these events virtually all of them shot. Other figures point in the same direction. One of the facts which influenced the passage of the Brady Bill in the USA was the information that handguns were held responsible for the sevenfold difference in the homicide rate between Vancouver, Canada and Seatle, USA despite the fact that the two cities had similar rates of assault (Sloan, Kellerman, Reay et al 1988). There will be more tragedies if restrictions are not introduced.

The case for handgun control is clear. There are bound to be a few people who have a predisposition to kill people and by making the means easily available we are clearly going to cause problems.

Adult roles to be available

As mentioned in Chapter 10 the Home Office researchers pointed to a link between lack of employment and crime. They argued that with the lack of proper jobs a higher proportion of young men were finding it difficult to make the transition to adulthood.

They advocate that the younger generation can be helped by jobs, training, better preparation for fatherhood, lessons for those with teenage children and temporary housing (Travis 1996c).

Final comments In the last resort there is a case for saying that society obtains the level of crime it deserves. If we wish to reduce the incidence of crime we need to change society. It is important to produce a sense of fairness where people have opportunities to develop but which values the contributing of all members of the society. Where people do not narrowly seek their own interests but realise the importance of helping those who are in trouble and support the weaker members of the community.

Table 2.1

Offenses of under age sex and Conceptions amongst under sixteens

	Conception rate per 1,000 aged under 16 years			Under age sex recorded by police (number).
	Total	Maternities	Abortion	
1985	8.6	3.8	4.8	2687
1989	9.4	4.5	4.9	2471
1990	10.1	5.0	5.1	2140
1991	9.3	4.6	4.8	1949
1992	8.5	4.2	4.3	1563
1993	8.1	3.9	4.2	1443

Source Francome 1995 and Home Office 1994 p51

Table 2.2

Evidence from Criminal Statistics
Notifiable offenses recorded by the police 1979-1994.

Number of offenses (Thousands)

	1979	1985	1992	1993	1994
Violence against the person	95.0	121.7	201.8	205.1	219.7
Sexual Offenses	21.8	21.5	29.5	31.3	32.0
Robbery	12.5	27.5	52.9	57.8	60.0
All violent crime	129.3	170.6	284.2	294.2	311.7
Burglary	544.0	866.7	1355.3	1369.6	1261.4
Theft (and handling)	1416.1	1884.1	2851.6	2751.9	2560.7
Fraud and forgery	118.0	134.8	168.6	162.8	146.2
Criminal damage including arson	320.5	539.0	892.6	906.7	930.4
Other notifiable offenses	8.8	16.7	39.4	41.0	47.7
Total	2536.7	3611.9	5591.7	5526.3	5258.1

Table 2.3

Notifiable offenses recorded by the police per 100,000 pop 1979-94.

	1979	1985	1992	1993	1994
Violence against the person	193	245	392	400	427
Sexual Offenses	44	43	58	61	62
Robbery	25	55	104	113	117
Burglary	1106	1742	2652	2671	2452
Theft (and handling)	2972 (80*)	3786	5581	5367	4978
Fraud and forgery	214 (80*)	271	330	318	284
Criminal damage including arson	730 (80*)	1083	1747	1768	1809
Other notifiable offenses	18	34	77	80	93
Total	5159	7258	10,943	10,777	10,222

Source Home Office 1995 p 40

Table 2.4

Clear up Rates

Clear up rates   Percentages and total number

	1979	1985	1992	1993	1994
Violence against the person	77	73	76	76	77
Sexual Offenses[1]	75	72	75	75	76
Robbery	31	22	22	22	22
Burglary	31	29	20	19	20
Theft (and handling)[2]	40	35	24	23	24
Fraud and forgery[2]	82	68	53	51	52
Criminal damage including arson[23]	30	23	17	16	17
Other notifiable[4] offenses	94	94	96	95	96
Total[3]	41%	35%	26%	25%	26%
Total in millions[3]	0.98	1.21	1.39	1.33	1.33

Home office 1988 p43 and 1994 p45

1 Includes offenses of gross indecency with a child from 1983.
2 Figure for 1979 is not comparable with later ones
3 Excludes 'other criminal damage' of value £20 and below.
4 1979 figure not comparable as from 1983 offenses 'trafficking in controlled drugs' was included.

Table 2.5

Clear up rate based on British Crime Survey Figures 1992.

Percentages

	Raw Clear up rate	Best estimate of % recorded	Adjusted clear up rate
Violence against the person	77	24	18%
Robbery	22	12	3%
Burglary	20	68	14%
Criminal damage including arson	17	14%	2%
Total	26%	27%	7%

Home Office 1994 p45 and 1995 p27 Mayhew et al 1993 p15

Table 2.6

Number of offenses initially recorded as homicide

	1979	1985	1992	1993	1994	1995
Total Offenses	629	625	682	675	729	746
Offenses no longer recorded as homicide		89	98	101	52	
Court decisions						
Murder	160	166	191	204	104	
Manslaughter	284	252	263	236	157	
Infanticide	7	8	6	4	2	
total	451	426	455	293	263	
Court decision due			4	28	274	
Number homicides per million*	11.1	10.7	11.6	11.8	12.7	13.0

<u>Source</u> Home Office 1995 p78

Table 2.7

Method of Killing of men and women in 1993/4

	Males 1994 No	%	1993 %	Females 1994 No	%	1993 %	All 1994 No	%	1993 %
Sharp instrument	165	41	36	71	26	26	236	35	32
Blunt instrument	33	8	11	23	9	13	56	8	12
Hitting kicking etc	74	18	20	37	14	13	111	16	17
Strangulation	31	8	8	75	28	27	106	16	16
Shooting	50	12	15	13	5	9	63	9	12
Explosion			1						1
Burning	23	6	2	19	7	3	42	6	2
Drowning	8	2	1	6	2	1	14	2	1
Poison or drugs	8	2	2	15	6	1	23	3	2
Motor vehicle	5	1	2	3	1	2	8	1	2
Other	6	1	3	2	1	3	8	1	3
Not known	6	1	1	6	2	1	10	1	1
Total	407	100	100	270	100	100	677	100	100

Source Home Office 1995 p79

Table 2.8

Relationship of victim to principal suspect in offenses recorded as homicide 1993

	Males No	%	Females No	%	All No	%
Victim acquainted						
Son or daughter	24	6	30	13	54	9
Parent	12	3	12	5	24	4
Spouse or cohabitant (or previous)	15	4	78	34	93	15
Other family	10	3	8	3	18	3
Lover or past lover	9	2	14	6	23	4
Friend or acquaintance	112	30	42	18	124	25
Other associate	20	5	3	1	23	4
Victim not acquainted	143	38	27	12	170	28
No suspect.	30	8	17	7	47	8
Total	375	100	231	100	606	100

Source Home Office (1994 p77/8)

Table 2.9

Rates of rape in Britain and the United States per 100,000 population

Year	Britain	USA
1973	2.0	24.5
1975	2.1	26.3
1977	2.1	29.1
1979	2.4	34.5
1981	2.2	35.6
1986	4.6	37.9
1992	8.2	42.8
1993	9.2	40.6
1995	9.9	

Table 2.10

Number of rapes in Britain recorded by the police

Thousands

Year	Rapes	Indecent assault on female
1979	1.2	11.8
1981	1.1	10.6
1986	2.3	11.8
1990	3.4	15.8
1992	4.1	16.2
1993	4.6	17.4
1995	5.1	

Source Criminal Statistics 1993 p37 and 1987 p29.

Table 2.11

Number of offenses recorded by the police in which firearms were reported to have been used by offence group

	1979	1985	1992	1993	1994
Total Offenses	6572	9742	13,305	13,951	12,977
Homicide	40	45	56	74	66
Robbery	1038	2531	5827	5918	4104
Burglary	80	125	182	235	255

Table 2.12
Crimes known to the police-main developed countries
Millions

	1987	1991	1992	1993	1994	% rise 87-94
England and Wales	3.89	5.28	5.59	5.53	5.26	35
Northern Ireland	0.06	0.06	0.07	0.07	0.07	6
Scotland	0.48	0.59	0.60	0.54	0.53	10
Ireland	0.09	0.09	0.10	0.10	0.10	18
France	3.17	3.74	3.83	3.88	3.92	24
Belgium	0.29	0.38	0.39	0.39	0.56*	..
Germany	4.44	5.30	6.29	6.75	6.54	16
Austria	0.39	0.47	0.50	0.49		26 ('93)
Netherlands	1.04	1.08	1.68	1.17	1.17	15
Norway	0.20	0.22	0.25	0.23	0.23	13
Sweden	0.95	1.05	1.05	1.03	0.98	3
Denmark	0.52	0.52	o.56	0.55	0.55	4
Finland	0.32	0.39	0.39	0.39	0.38	21
Portugal	0.25	0.31	0.33	0.31	0.33*	..
Italy	1.87	2.65	2.39	2.25	2.17	16
Greece	0.30	0.36	0.38	0.36	0.30	0
USA	13.51	14.87	14.44	14.1		5 ('93)
Canada	2.37	2.90	2.85	2.7	2.6	11
Japan	1,58	1.71	1.74	1.8		14 ('93)
Australia	1.07	1.27	1.27	..		..
New Zealand	0.41	0.48	0.45	0.5	0.5	20

Source Home Office 1994 p23

Table 2.13
Prison Population by European Country

	1987	1992	1993	Per 100,000 Population	Per 100,000 recorded crime
England & Wales	47,105	46,350	45,633	89	830
Northern Ireland	1858	1811	1902	118	2870
Scotland	5421	5361	5900	115	1090
Rep of Ireland	1936	2155	2108	60	2130
France	50,639	49,323	51,134	86	1320
Belgium	6713	7116	7203	72	1860
Germany	51,919		65,838	81	1975
Austria	7419	6913	7099	89	1440
Netherlands	5002	7297	8037	77	685
Norway	1929		2607	60	1050
Sweden	4198	5431	5794	66	560
Denmark	3190	3406	3702	71	680
Finland	3824	3295	3132	62	811
Portugal	8270	9183	11,079	112	3605
Italy	34,838	46,152	51,231	88	2258
Greece	3988	6252	6524	68	1820

Source Home Office 1995 p24.

Table 2.14

Changes in prison population compared to changes in crime. Selected countries 1987-93.

	% increase prison pop	% increase in known crimes	% increase in violent crime	
			1987-94	1993-94
Greece	64%	18%	17%	4%
Netherlands	61%	13%	59%	7%
Italy	46%	21%	5%	-3%
Sweden	38%	9%	52%	2%
Norway	35%	25%	..	..%
Portugal	32%	..	..	8%
Scotland	9%	13%	9%	1%
Rep of Ireland	9%	16%	19%	0%
Northern Ireland	2%	4%	2%	2%
England and Wales	-3%	42%	57%	6%
Finland	-18%	22%	19%	6%

Source Home Office 1994 p23 and 24)

Table 7.1
Teenage pregnancy rates by year for England and Wales

	All Teenagers			Under sixteens		
Year	Conception rate per 1,000 aged 15-19 yrs			Conception rate per 1,000 aged 13-15 yrs		
	Total	Maternities	abortion	Total	Maternities	Abortion
1980	58.7	40.5	18.2	7.2	3.3	3.9
1985	61.7	40.8	20.9	8.6	3.8	4.8
1989	67.6	43.5	24.0	9.4	4.5	4.9
1990	69.0	44.4	24.6	10.1	5.0	5.1
1991	65.1	42.7	22.4	9.3	4.6	4.8

Sources OPCS 1993 and 1994a.

Table 7.2
Quality of sex education received by the young mothers

Subject	No Information		Little Information		Good Information	
Periods	16	13.6%	55	46.6%	47	39.8%
Pregnancy	33	28.0%	60	50.8%	25	21.2%
HIV	48	41.0%	44	35.8%	31	25.2%
Condoms	36	30.8%	48	41.0%	33	28.2%
Other BC	36	30.5%	54	45.8%	28	23.7%
Relationships	46	37.4%	53	43.1%	14	11.4%

Table 7.3
Reasons for first experience of sexual intercourse

Motivating factor	Age 14 & 15		Age 16 & 17		All	
In love	47	66.2%	27	50.9%	74	59.7%
Curiosity	15	21.1%	20	37.7%	35	28.2%
Pressure from partner	1	1.4%	8	15.1%	9	7.3%
Drunk	9	12.7%	5	9.4%	14	11.3%
Rape	4	5.6%	0	0.0%	4	3.2%
Wanted to get pregnant	1	1.4%	1	1.9%	2	1.6%
All my friends were doing it	10	14.1%	7	13.2%	17	13.7%
Got carried away	21	29.5%	15	28.3%	36	29.0%
To please my partner	11	15.5%	5	9.4%	16	12.9%
To find out about it	12	16.9%	14	26.4%	26	21.0%
Total number	71		53		124	

Table 7.4
Age of woman and partner at first intercourse

Those aged 14 &15   Those aged 16 &17

Age	Age at which girls first had intercourse		Partner's age		Age of first intercourse for 16/17yrs		Partner's age	
11	1	1.4%						
12	6	8.5%			4	7.1%	1	1.8%
13	16	22.5%			13	23.2%	1	1.8%
14	38	53.5%	7	10.4%	21	37.5%	3	5.3%
15	10	14.1%	15	22.4%	14	25.0%	10	17.9%
16			10	14.9%	4	7.1%	9	16.1%
17			13	19.4%			7	12.5%
18			6	9.0%			10	17.9%
19			4	6.0%			7	12.5%
20+			12	17.9%			8	14.3%
Total	71	100%	67	100%	56	100%	56	100%

Table 7.5
Birth control use at first intercourse

Method	Aged 14 & 15		Aged 16 and 17		All	%
Pill	3	4.3%	4	7.3%	7	5.6%
Condom	31	44.9%	24	43.6%	55	44.4%
Withdrawal	4	5.8%	4	7.3%	8	6.5%
None used	31	44.9%	23	41.8%	54	43.5%

Table 7.6
Age of teenagers and their partners at pregnancy.

Partner's Age

Girls age	14	15	16	17	18	19	20	21	22	23	24	25	27
13		5	2	2	1	1	1			1	1		
14	5	5	5	12	6	5		4	1		2	2	
15	2	5	7	11	6	9	4	2	2	3	1	1	2
16		1		1	2		1			2			
17								1	1				
All	7	16	14	26	15	15	6	7	4	.6	4	3	2

Note In addition to the table one young woman became pregnant at the age of twelve and her partner was aged fifteen years.

Table 8.1

Planning according to initial meeting place

Place	Planned		partially planned		explosive	
Victim's home	111	(66%)	3	2%	54	32%
Other place	38	75%	3	6%	10	19%
offender's home	34	83%	1	2%	6	15%
On the street	201	71%	55	20%	25	9%
In or just outside a bar	54	77%	10	14%	6	9%
Picnic, park or party	19	86%	1	5%	2	9%
Total	457	72%	73	12%	103	16%

Note Total only comes to 633 as in thirteen cases no information on planning was available. Adapted from Amir 1971 p142.

Table 9.1

	1981	1991
Percentage of employed work force in manufacturing	26%	18%
Female participation in the work force	30%	45%
Estimated number of households with separated parents	570,000	1,300,000
Owner-occupier households as a percentage of total	56%	68%

Bibliography

Abrahamsen D (1960) The psychology of Crime New York, John Wiley.

Allcorn D (1955) The Social Development of Young Men in an English Industrial Suburb Unpublished PhD thesis Manchester University.

Amir M (1971) Patterns in Forcible rape University of Chicago Press.

Anderson Henry (1967) 'The case against the drug culture' Peace News 17th March.

Bates Stephen (1994) 'Howard leads vote against hanging return' The Guardian Feb 22 p6 col 7.

Becker H (1951) 'The professional dance musician and his audience' American Journal of Sociology 1951 p136-44.

Becker H (1963) The Outsiders New York, Free Press.

Beresford David (1987) Ten Men Dead Grafton Press.

Beresford David (1995) 'Anti Crime blitz shows Mandella means business' The Guardian 25th July p10 col 6.

Berrueta-Clement JR, Schweinhart LJ, Barnett et al (1984) 'Changed lives: the effect of the Perry preschool programme of youths through age 19' Ypsilanti, MI High/Scope.

Blair Tony (1996) 'A stakehold Society' Fabian Review.Feb p1-4

Blair Tony (1996a) 'Why I am a Christian' Sunday Telegraph Review p1 col 1. 7 April.

Blake Pamela (1974) The plight of One parent Families London Council for Child Welfare.

Boseley Sarah (1996) 'Equal rights urged for unmarried fathers' The Guardian 1 May section 1 p5 col 1.

Brindle David (1994) 'Oasis benefit "will not buy children a workhouse Diet".' #the Guardian 1 Feb p5 col 1.

Brown Derek (1996) 'Peace Blown to Shreds' The Guardian p1 col1.

Brownmiller S (1975) Against our will: Men, Women and Rape New York, Bantam.

Burt Cyril (1925) The Young Delinquent University of London Press.
         Page numbers from 4th edition 1944.
Burghes L (1993) One parent families: policy options for the 1990s Family Policy Studies Institute and Joseph Rowtree Foundation.

Bugliosi Vincent with Gentry Curt (1977 ed) Helter Skelter Penguin edition, Harmondsworth.

Campbell Duncan (1996) 'Muggings rise during crackdown' TheGuardian 1 March p6 col7.

Cavendish M (1992) Serial Murderers WH Smith Ltd London.

Carson P and Martell M (1979) Children referred to closed units London DHSS

Central Statistical Office Regional Trends 29 London HMSO 1994.

Central Statistical Office Social Trends 11 London HMSO 1981.

Central Statistical Office Social Trends 25 London HMSO 1995.

Chancer L S (1987) 'New Bedford, Massachusetts, March 6th 1983-March 22 1984: The before and after of a group rape' Gender and Society, 1,239-260.

Chesney K (1970) The Victorian Underworld Temple Smith London.

Cohen S (1972) Folk Devils and Moral Panics London: Macgibbon and Kee.

Cohen S (1976) ed Images of Deviance Harmonsworth Penguin

Cohn N (1978) The Pursuit of the Millenium Palladin.

Coleman (1973) Transition to Adulthood US Government publication.

Criminal Law Revision Committee (1984) Prostitution in the Street sixteenth report CMND 9329 HMSO.

Davey Smith G and Eggar M (1993) 'Socioeconomic differentials in wealth and income'. BMJ vol 308 p705.

Department of Health (1991) On the State of Public Health London HMSO.

Department of Social Security (1993) 'Households Below Average income: A statisticaal analysis' 1979-91, HMSO, London.

Dewar J (1989) Law and the Family Butterworths London and Edinburgh.

Downes D M (1966) The Delinquent Solution Routledge London.

Durkheim Emile (1897) Suicide Routlege London 1952 edition.

Farrell K (1980) Northern Ireland: the Orange State Pluto Press.

Forwell GD (1993) 'Glasgow's health: old problems-new opportunities', Department of Public Health: Glaasgow.

Foster K, Jackson B, Hunter M, Hunter P and Bennett N (1995) General Houshold Survey 1993 London HMSO.

Francome C (1976) Youth and Society University of Kent, Canterbury.

Francome C (1984) Abortion Freedom Unwin Hyman London and Boston.

Francome C (1986) Abortion Practice Unwin Hyman London and Boston.

Francome C and Wharton R (1973) 'An international social index' New Internationalist September, pp19-21.

Francome C, Churchill H, Savage W and Lewison H (1993) Caesarean Birth in Britain Middlesex UP London.

Francome C and Marx David (1996) Improving the Health of the Nation Middlesex University Press, London.

Freedland Jonathan (1996) 'Right smirks as Dole smiles' The Observer 18th August section A p21 col 1.

Ginsberg Morris On the Diversity of Morals William Heinemann Ltd, London 1956.

Glueck B C Jnr (1956) New York Final Report on Deviant Sexual Offenders Albany New York Department of Mental Hygiene.

Goodman A and Webb S (1994) For Richer for Poorer Joseph Rowntree Foundation London.

Gouldner A (1971) The Coming Crisis of Western Sociology Heinemann London.

Heath E (1993) 'Tomorrow is a better day' The Guardian 18 Nov p24 col 3.

Heath I (1994) 'The poor man at his gaate' BMJ Vol 309 pp1675-6.

Hirst P Q 'Marx and Engels on law, crime and morality' in Taylor I, Walton P and Young J (1975) Critical Criminology Routledge, London.

Hockreich and Rotter J of Personality and Social Psychology' 1970 pp 211-214.

Home Office (1980) Criminal Statistics England and Wales 1979 HMSO London.

Home Office (1988) Criminal Statistics England and Wales 1987 HMSO London.

Home Office (1994) Criminal Statistics England and Wales 1993 HMSO London.

Home Office (1995) Criminal Statistics England and Wales 1994 HMSO

Johnson DL, Walker T (1987) 'Primary prevention of behaviour problems in Mexican-American children' Am J Community Psychol vol 15 375-385.

Katz Ian and Cohen Nick (1996) 'Can we heed big Apple's Message' The Observer 2 June Focus p18 col 1.

Lally JR, Mangione PL, Honig AS et al (1988) 'More pride, less delinquency: findings from the ten-year follow-up study of the Syracuse University family development research programme Zero to three April 13-8.

Lauter P and Howe F (1970) The conspiracy of the Young World Publishing.

Leary Tim (1968) The Politics of Ecstacy GP Putnam's Sons.

Levine R (1959) 'Gusii sex offences: a study in social control' American Anthropologist Vol 61.

Lewis C (1992) 'Crime statistics: their use and misuse' Social Trends 22 p13-23 Central Statistical Office HMSO London.

Lindsey B (1925) The revolt of modern youth Boni and Liveright.

Littner N (1973) 'Psychology of the sex offender: Causes, treatment, prognosis'. Police Law Quarterly 3, 5-31.

Macardle D (1937) 'The Irish Republic Corgi Book ed 1968, London.

Martin David (1967) A Sociology of English Religion Heinnmann.

Marx K Capital Pelican ed 1976 vol 1

Marx K and Engels F (1848) Communist Manifesto Penguin edition 1967 Middlesex

Marx K and Engels F (1844) The German Ideology 1974 edition Lawrence and Wishart London edited by C J Arthur.

Matthews R (1986) 'Beyond Wolfendon? Prostitution, politics and the law' in Matthews and Young J Confronting Crime Sage London.

Matthews R and Young J (1986) Confronting Crime Sage London.

Matza David (1964) Delinquency and Drift John Wiley and Sons London and New York.

Matza D amd Sykes G (1957) 'Juvenile Delinquency and Subterranea Values' American Sociological Review No 26 p712-19.

McClintock T (1995) 'Creating New Criminals' BMJ vol 311 p1037 21 October.

McKie David 'Four in 10 Consevatives opposed change' The Guardian 23 February 1994 p2 col 4.

Mead Margaret (1944) The American Troops and the British Community Hutchinson.

Mead M (1970) Culture and Commitment Penguin, London.

Mellor Kay 'Legalised brothels won't save prostitutes from the pimps' The Observer 3rd August 1996 p3.

Milham S, Bullock R, Hosie K (1978) Locking up children Dartington, Dartington Social Research Institute.

Mills H and Arlidge J (1996) 'Labour pledges gun ban after Tory ruse misfires' The Guardian 4th August p5 col 1.

Morgan P (1995) Farewell to the Family Institute of Economic Affairs, London.

Olds DL, Henderson CR, Chamberlain R and Tatelbaum R (1986) 'Preventing child abuse and neglect: arandomised trial of nurse home visitation' Paediatrics vol 78 pp54-78.

Oppenheim C (1993) Poverty the Facts Child Poverty Action Group, London.

Orwell G (1944) The English People in Orwell Sonia and Angus Ian (eda) The collected Essays, jounalism and letters of George Orwell Vol 3 London Secker and Warburg.

O'Toole Fintan (1996) 'Ireland's Easter Charade' The Observer 7 April The Review p1 Col 1.

Rigby Andrew (1974) Alternative Realities Routledge London.

Roberts K (1985) Youth and Leisure Allen and Unwin London.

Roiphe K (1994) The Morning After Little Brown and co. London, NY and Boston.

Rose D 'Convictions Plummet under Tories' The Observer 21 January 1996 p1 Column One and P16 col 1.

Salgado G (1995) The Elizabethan Underworld Alan Sutton publishing Stroud Glos.

Sanday PG (1979) 'The socio-cultural context of Rape'. Washington DC US Department of Commerce, National Technical information Service.

Schur E (1965) Crimes without Victims Prentice Hall, Englewood Cliffs NJ.

Schur E and Bedau H A (1974) Victimless Crimes Prentice Hall, Englewood Cliffs, NJ.

Sharrock David 'The troubles with Gerry' The Guardian 15 Feb Section 2 p2 col 1.

Sheffield Emily 'Friend in Need' The Guardian 15 August 1996 p13 col 1.

Shepherd Jonathon P and Farrington David P (1995) 'Preventing crime and violence' BMJ 4 Feb 1995 pp171-2.

Silverman I and Dinitz S (974) Compulsive Masculinity and Delinquency: an empirical investigation' Criminology 11 p498-515.#

Sloan JH, Kellerman AL, Reay DT et al (1988) N Engl J Med vol 319 1256-62.

Smellie KB (1955) The British Way of Life London, Heinemann.

Smith R and Leaning J (1993) 'Medicine and Global Survival' British Medical Journal Vol 307-pp693-4.

Taylor I (1981) Law and Order: arguments for Socialism:

Taylor I, Walton P and Young J (1973) The New Criminology Routledge, London.

Taylor I, Walton P and Young J (1975) Critical Criminology Routledge, London.

Thatcher M (1993) The Downing Street years Harper Collins London.

Thomas R 'UK Worst in rich and poor divide' The Guardian 28th October 1995 p2 col 3.

Titmuss R M (1966) Essays on the Welfare State Unwin University Books

Toner B (1982) The facts of Rape Arrow Books London

Townsend Peter (1996) 'Stakeholder Welfare' Fabian Review.Feb p5,6.

Travis (1996a) 'Muggings mar third year's fall in crime' Guardian 27 March 1996 p4 col 4.

Travis (1996b) 'Defensive PM attacks crime leak' Guardian 1 May 1996 p2 col 7.

Travis (1996c) 'Young turn to "career crime" ' The Guardian 19 January p1 col1.

Trevelyan G M (1970) English Social History Pelican Middlesex.

Utting David (1994) Title Fabian Society London.

Walker Martin 'US tries to heal a wounded peace' The Guardian 5th March 1996 p11.

Walker Martin (1996a) 'Sweet Talk leaves the women cold' The Observer 18 August section one p21 col 7

Wardlaw Grant (1989) Political Terrorism Cambridge UP.

West DJ (1978) Understaninding Sexual Attacks Heinemann London.

White Michael 'Gay consent "will return to the Commons".' The Guardian 22 February 1994 p6 col 1.

Whitehead M Inequalities in Health Penguin, london 1992.

Wightman J (1979a) 'Mrs Thatcher and Whitelaw disagree over hanging' Daily Telegraph 26 April p10 col A.

Wightman J (1979b) 'Thatcher Buoyant' <u>Daily Telegraph</u> 1 May p36 col D.

Wightman J (1979c) 'Thatcher Freedom Call' <u>Daily Telegraph</u> 2 May p36 col F.

Wilkinson RG (1986) 'Income and Mortality' in <u>Class and Health: Research and Lontitudinal data</u> ed Wilkinson Tavistock Press London.

Wilkinson RG (1992) 'Income distribution and life expectancy' <u>BMJ</u> vol 304 pp165-8.

Wilkinson RG (1994) <u>Unfarid Shares</u> Barnado's London.

Williams GH (1962) <u>The Radical Reformation</u> Westminster Press.

Williams K S (1994) <u>Criminology</u> Blackstone Press ltd, London.

Willis P (1977) <u>Learning to Labour</u> Saxon House, London.

Wilson James Q and Herrnstein RJ (1985) <u>Crime and Human Nature</u> Simon and Schuster New York

Wright Giles (1981) <u>Facts for Socialists</u> Fabian Society, London.

Yinger JM (1960) 'Contraculture' <u>American Sociological Review</u> October pp 625-635.

Young Jock (1968) Ph D thesis Lodon University (under WS Young).

Young Jock (1971) <u>he Drugtakers</u> Paladin London.

Young J (1973) <u>The manufacture of news: Deviance.Social Problems and the Media</u> London, Constable.

Young J (1975) 'Working Class Criminology' in Taylor I, Walton P and Young J <u>Critical Criminology</u> Routledge, London.